STANLEY®

Basic
Plumbing
PRO TIPS AND SIMPLE STEPS

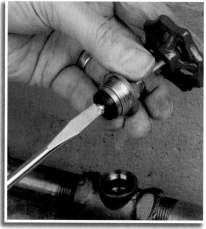

Meredith® Books
Des Moines, Iowa

Stanley® Books
An imprint of Meredith® Books

Stanley Basic Plumbing
Editor: Ken Sidey
Senior Associate Design Director: Tom Wegner
Assistant Editor: Harijs Priekulis
Copy Chief: Terri Fredrickson
Copy and Production Editor: Victoria Forlini
Editorial Operations Manager: Karen Schirm
Managers, Book Production: Pam Kvitne,
    Marjorie J. Schenkelberg
Technical Editors, The Stanley Works: Mike Maznio
Contributing Copy Editor: Kim Catanzarite
Technical Proofreader: George Granseth
Contributing Proofreaders: Raymond L. Kast, Jim Stepp,
    Kathy Roth Eastman
Electronic Production Coordinator: Paula Forest
Editorial and Design Assistants: Renee E. McAtee,
    Karen McFadden

Additional Editorial Contributions from
    Greenleaf Publishing
Publishing Director: Dave Toht
Writer: Steve Cory
Production Designer: Rebecca Anderson
Associate Designer: Jean DeVaty
Editorial Assistant: Betony Toht
Photography: Dan Stultz, Stultz Photography
Illustrator: Dave Brandon, Art Rep Services
Studio Assistant: Tom Maloney
Technical Consultant: Joe Hansa
Indexer: Nan Badgett

Meredith® Books
Publisher and Editor in Chief: James D. Blume
Design Director: Matt Strelecki
Managing Editor: Gregory H. Kayko
Executive Editor, Gardening and Home Improvement:
    Benjamin W. Allen
Executive Editor, Home Improvement: Larry Erickson

Director, Operations: George A. Susral
Director, Production: Douglas M. Johnston
Vice President and General Manager: Douglas J. Guendel

Meredith Publishing Group
President, Publishing Group: Stephen M. Lacy
Vice President-Publishing Director: Bob Mate

Meredith Corporation
Chairman and Chief Executive Officer: William T. Kerr
Chairman of the Executive Committee: E.T. Meredith III

Thanks to
B. T. Premier Plumbing, Inc.

All of us at Stanley® Books are dedicated to providing you with the information and ideas you need to enhance your home and garden. We welcome your comments and suggestions about this book. Write to us at:
Meredith Corporation
Stanley Books
1716 Locust St. LN-118
Des Moines, IA 50309–3023

If you would like more information on other Stanley products, call 1-800-STANLEY or visit us at: www.stanleyworks.com Stanley® and the notched rectangle around the Stanley name are registered trademarks of The Stanley Works and subsidiaries.

If you would like to purchase any of our home improvement, cooking, crafts, gardening, or home decorating and design books, check wherever quality books are sold. Or visit us at: meredithbooks.com

Note to the Readers: Due to differing conditions, tools, and individual skills, Meredith Corporation assumes no responsibility for any damages, injuries suffered, or losses incurred as a result of following the information published in this book. Before beginning any project, review the instructions carefully, and if any doubts or questions remain, consult local experts or authorities. Because codes and regulations vary greatly, you always should check with authorities to ensure that your project complies with all applicable local codes and regulations. Always read and observe all of the safety precautions provided by manufacturers of any tools, equipment, or supplies, and follow all accepted safety procedures.

CONTENTS

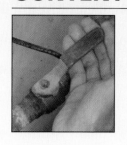

PLUMBING PREPARATION

One look at the tangle of pipes and valves under a kitchen sink is usually enough to make a homeowner reach for the phonebook to find a professional plumber. At first glance, the work seems both difficult and messy. However, many plumbing repairs and installations are surprisingly homeowner-friendly.

The scope of the book

This book helps you save money by teaching you to do the work yourself. It walks you through common plumbing repairs and teaches you how to replace existing sinks, faucets, toilets, and related appliances. Running new plumbing lines and installing fixtures where none exist, however, are beyond the scope of this book. Consult a plumbing professional for projects of that scope.

Know your limits

If you are handy, all the projects in this book are well within your reach. This chapter will give you a basic understanding of a plumbing system and tell you which tools you need.

Plan your time carefully; your family will not be able to use a plumbing fixture until you have finished the repair or installation. The "Prestart Checklist" at the beginning of each project will help you gather the needed tools and estimate the time needed to complete the project.

Even a well planned project can run into unforeseen problems, and you may find yourself in need of tools or parts, so do your work while the stores are open.

Working safely and comfortably

Before attempting any project, turn off the water and turn on a faucet to make sure the water supply is off.

Take care not to touch nearby electrical outlets, especially if you are wet.

Plumbing is sometimes physically challenging, not because of heavy lifting but because you often have to work in cramped conditions. Use knee pads and even an old pillow (page 19) to make the work area more comfortable. Spread drop cloths around to catch water and the grime of old pipes and fittings.

Essential repairs and upgrades require only a modest set of tools and some basic knowledge.

CHAPTER PREVIEW

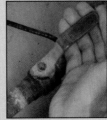
Shutting off the water
page 6

Plumbing tools
page 8

Drain, waste, vent system
page 10

Supply system
page 12

Accessibility is often the most difficult aspect of plumbing. When you remove the pedestal on a pedestal sink (above), it's easy to get to the trap, drain body, and supply tubes. A bathroom sink in a vanity or a kitchen sink can be much more awkward.

Pipes and fittings
page 14

Common plumbing system problems
page 16

SHUTTING OFF THE WATER

It's the basic prerequisite for most plumbing projects: Shut off the water to the work area, then test to make sure the water supply is shut off. Failing to shut off the water leads to the sort of disaster you see in the comics: water spraying uncontrollably all over the place.

Every adult family member should know how to shut water off, both at the fixtures and to the entire house.

Fixture shutoffs

Most homes built in the past 40 years have a separate stop valve (also called a fixture shutoff valve) for each faucet, toilet, and fixture. A supply tube (sometimes called a riser) runs from the stop valve to the fixture. (A faucet has two stop valves, one for hot water and one for cold; a toilet needs only a cold-water shutoff.) If a fixture does not have a stop valve, you will have to shut off water to part or all of the house before working. It's a good idea to install a stop valve so you can stop the flow quickly in case of emergency *(pages 110–111).*

A stop valve typically has a chrome finish and an oval handle. In an older home, it may be shaped like a house valve with a circular handle, or it may have a decorative ceramic handle.

Most stop valves are inexpensive and made for light duty because they will be used only for emergencies or repairs. That means they might not shut off the water completely. Do not crank down on its handle with pliers; you may break the valve. See *pages 108–109* to repair a faulty stop valve or supply tube.

Main shutoffs

Every home has at least one main shutoff, which controls water flowing to the entire house. Often there is one main shutoff inside the house and another outside.

An inside main shutoff is usually located near the point where water enters the house. Often it is near the water meter. There may be two valves, one on each side of the meter. If your home has no meter (some homes don't), look for a large pipe that enters the house, often through a basement floor or at the bottom of a crawlspace. The shutoff should be somewhere along the run of that pipe.

In regions that experience mild winters, the main shutoff valve may be located outside of the house.

Stop valves

Kitchen sink stop valves often are hidden amid the jumble of pipes and tubes under the sink. Stop valves allow you to shut off water to the kitchen faucet. There may be a separate stop valve for the dishwasher.

A saddle tee-valve tied into a supply pipe runs cold water to a refrigerator's ice maker. Although a saddle tee is a handy way to tap into a line, some municipalities forbid its use. Check local building codes.

In-faucet stop valves can be found on some tub/shower faucets. Use a large slot screwdriver to turn water on and off.

An outside shutoff valve is located near the point where a pipe branches off from the utility's main line to bring water to your home. If you have a parkway—a narrow strip of land between the sidewalk and the street—the outside shutoff will likely be found there. If you cannot find yours, ask your municipality where to find it.

In temperate regions, an outside shutoff is usually housed in a plastic or concrete underground container, sometimes called a Buffalo box (below). Usually the box lid can be pried up, but you may need to dig away vegetation to free it.

In colder regions, the shutoff will be below the frost line, typically at the bottom of a tube covered with a cast-iron cover. It may be necessary to buy a "key" to be able to reach down to the valve and turn the water on and off. Keys are usually the same size and type throughout a neighborhood. Often your municipality will let you borrow a key for your shutoff.

Intermediate shutoffs
You may find other shutoff valves located on exposed supply pipes in a basement, crawlspace, utility room, or access panel behind a bathtub *(page 12)*. These will probably be in pairs, one for hot and one for cold water. (If the water has been running recently, you can tell which pipe is hot by feeling them with your hand.) These are probably intermediate shutoffs, meaning they control water supply to a portion of a house.

To find out what a shutoff valve controls, close it and go through the house turning on faucets and flushing toilets. Remember that a toilet with a tank will flush once after the water is off; listen or look for water refilling the tank after the flush.

If you have hot-water heat in your home, there will be shutoff valves near the boiler. These have nothing to do with the supply pipes for your plumbing fixtures.

Water meters
To keep track of water usage or to check that the utility is charging correctly, read your water meter. If your meter has a series of dials, each is labeled for the number of cubic feet it measures. It may be that some dials turn counterclockwise while others turn clockwise. A meter with a digital readout simply displays the amount of cubic feet of water used. Note the number at the start of the month or billing period, then read it again at the end and subtract the first number to calculate your use.

Shutoff valves

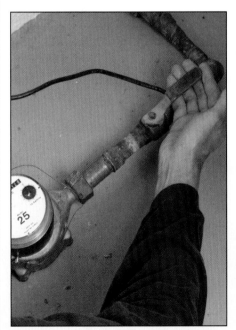

An in-house main shutoff, a fairly large valve located near the point where water enters the house, shuts water off for the entire house. As shown above, the shutoff valve is located next to the water meter.

A Buffalo box is another type of whole-house shutoff. Common in the South and Southwest, this buried box can be found outdoors. Pry off the lid. Inside you'll find either a standard valve that you can turn with your hands or one that requires a special key.

Intermediate shutoff valves control water flow to part of the house. There will be two or more pairs of these.

PLUMBING TOOLS

Buying a set of plumbing tools to suit your needs will probably cost less than one visit from a plumber. Purchase good-quality rather than bargain-bin tools, so you can be confident they will perform when needed.

Basic tools

To be prepared for clogs in sinks, toilets, and tubs, have on hand a **flanged plunger,** which has a funnel-like extension that fits snugly into a toilet. To plunge a sink or tub, fold up the flange or use a **standard plunger** without a flange. A **pressure plunger,** which expels a burst of water, sometimes can clear clogs that standard plungers can't handle.

When plunging does not clear a clog, use a **hand-crank drum auger,** also called a snake. A **toilet auger** fits into the toilet and has a sleeve to protect the bowl's porcelain finish.

To grip pipes and fittings, purchase a pair of top-quality **groove-joint pliers.** A 12-inch pair is the most useful size. Tighten or loosen nuts and fittings without marring them by using use an **adjustable wrench.** A **pipe wrench** bites into pipes and fittings for a sure grip and offers plenty of leverage. If you need to deal with steel pipe (either galvanized water pipe or black gas pipe), buy two pipe wrenches.

Plumbing often requires that you squeeze into dark places; a **flashlight** helps, especially one that stands and swivels.

Hand-crank drum auger

Pipe wrench

Putty knife

Toilet auger

Adjustable wrench

Flanged plunger

Pressure plunger

Standard plunger

Groove-joint pliers

Standard screwdriver

4-in-1 screwdriver

Flashlight

STANLEY PRO TIP

Buy a basin wrench

Without this tool, removing a kitchen or bathroom faucet is difficult, if not impossible. A basin wrench reaches into small spaces to grab a hold-down nut and loosen or tighten it.

Common carpenter tools often come into play during plumbing projects. A **4-in-1 screwdriver** will handle most jobs. You may need a **hammer** and a standard **screwdriver** to loosen stuck parts. A **tape measure** is indispensible for measuring pipe runs; use a **torpedo level** to position fixtures. A **putty knife** is handy for applying plumber's putty.

Specialized tools
A tool designed for a specific task is often worth the cost. For example, if an old faucet handle is stuck, prying it loose with a screwdriver may break it. A **handle puller** is easier to use and less risky. To replace the stem on a compression-type faucet, a **seat wrench** makes the job easy.

A **tubing cutter** is the best tool to cut copper pipe. For steel pipe, use a **hacksaw**. (Small versions of these tools make it easier to cut old pipe in tight spots.) A **plastic pipe cutter** deals with PVC or CPVC piping quickly. To sweat copper pipe and fittings *(pages 98–101)*, you'll need a **propane torch;** one with an electric lighter is easier to use than one that requires a match or striker. Prepare copper pipe with a **pipe brush** and **emery cloth**. If you plan to use flexible copper tubing, a **tubing bender** will enable you to bend it without kinking it.

When removing the basket strainer from a kitchen sink, use a **spud wrench** to remove the large-diameter hold-down nut.

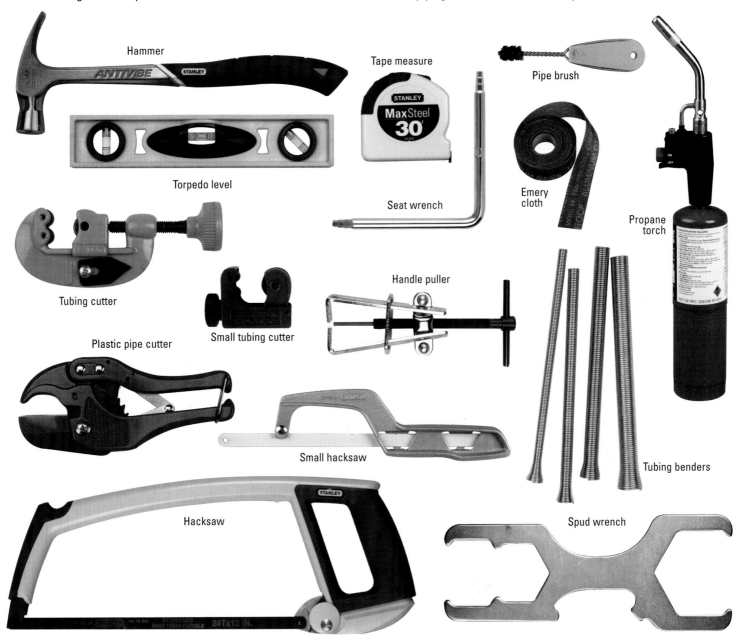

Hammer

Tape measure

Pipe brush

Torpedo level

Seat wrench

Emery cloth

Propane torch

Tubing cutter

Handle puller

Plastic pipe cutter

Small tubing cutter

Small hacksaw

Tubing benders

Hacksaw

Spud wrench

DRAIN, WASTE, VENT SYSTEM

Drain-waste-vent (DWV) pipes carry waste and water out of the house without gurgles or fumes. Never install or replace a DWV pipe without consulting a building inspector. These pipes must be installed according to precise specifications.

Drain pipes

The centerpiece of a DWV system is the **main stack,** usually a pipe 3 or 4 inches in diameter, which runs straight up through the roof. A **secondary stack**, perhaps 2 or 3 inches in diameter, serves a branch of the system.

Branch drain pipes of smaller diameter—typically 1½ or 2 inches—carry water from specific fixtures to a stack.

Drain stacks in older homes are often made of cast iron, which rusts through after 80 years or so. In older homes, the branch drains typically are made of galvanized steel, which is much more likely to rust and corrode shut. In newer homes, plastic pipe is used for stacks and branch drains. The first plastic pipe to be used was ABS, which is black. Since the 1970s, ABS has generally been replaced by white- or cream-colored PVC pipe. In rare cases, drain pipes are made of copper.

Drain pipes must be sloped so water runs freely through them, usually about ¼ inch per foot. Codes require special fittings make sweeping turns rather than abrupt turns, so waste does not get trapped in the pipes.

Drain pipes often have **cleanouts**—places where a plug can be temporarily removed—so the pipes can be augered to clear a clog.

The main drain line

Water travels downward through the stacks to the main drain line, which leads to the municipal sewage system or to a septic system. In older homes, the main drain may be made of clay pipe or other porous material. Tree roots sometimes work their way into the main line, causing wastewater to back up into the house. The solution is to call a company that specializes in augering main lines.

Vent pipes

For water to flow smoothly, without gurgling, there must be an air passageway behind the water (see below). Vent pipes extend from the drain pipes up through the roof to provide that passage. Vent pipes also carry odors out of the house.

The drain pipe for each plumbing fixture must be connected to a vent that supplies the pipe with air from the outside. In some cases, the drain pipe is connected directly to a main or secondary stack pipe, which travels straight up through the roof. More often, a drain pipe is connected to a **revent** pipe that reaches up and over to tie into the main vent stack.

Plumbing codes strictly prescribe where vent pipes can connect to the stack and how far they should travel. In most cases, a "wet" section of pipe—the part that carries wastewater—cannot be used as a vent, even if it is usually dry. Examine the illustration on the opposite page, and you'll see that all the vent pipes lead to sections of a stack that never carry running water.

If your drain pipes gurgle when you run water in a sink or flush a toilet, call a professional plumber for an inspection. A vent may be stopped up and need clearing. Or the plumbing may be incorrect, and you may need a new vent line.

In some cases, local codes allow for other venting strategies. For instance, a basement sink might be vented with a special wall vent, which simply runs out the wall. Or a cheater vent, a small device that draws air from the room rather than outside, may be allowed.

Why venting is necessary

Try to quickly empty a bottle with a narrow mouth, and it will gurgle and glug as it slowly empties. Open the vent cap on a plastic gas container and it flows smoothly. That's because the vent hole allows air to enter behind the flowing liquid, producing a quick, glug-free flow. Vent stacks in a household plumbing system work the same way.

Air trapped

Vent open

Irregular flow

Smooth flow

FIXTURE TRAPS

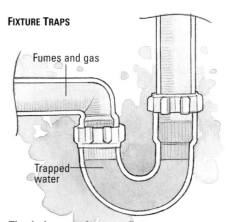

Fumes and gas

Trapped water

The drain water for every fixture must run through a trap—a section of pipe shaped like a sideways P or an S. Because of its shape, it holds water, creating a seal that keeps fumes and gases from entering the house. A toilet has a built-in trap. Sink traps are made of chrome-plated brass or plastic with joints that can easily be taken apart.

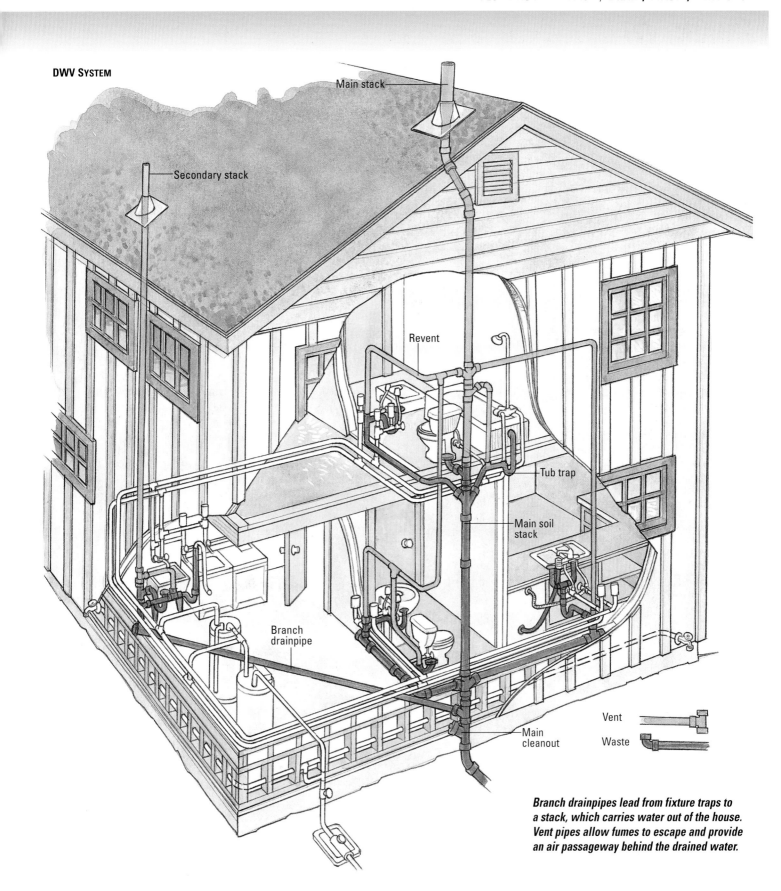

DWV SYSTEM

Main stack

Secondary stack

Revent

Tub trap

Main soil stack

Branch drainpipe

Vent

Waste

Main cleanout

Branch drainpipes lead from fixture traps to a stack, which carries water out of the house. Vent pipes allow fumes to escape and provide an air passageway behind the drained water.

SUPPLY SYSTEM

Pipes that carry water into the house are less complicated than the drain-waste-vent (DWV) pipes. Typically a single pipe runs to the water heater, where it divides into cold and hot pipes that supply faucets, fixtures, and toilets. Shutoff and stop valves make it possible to turn off the water along the supply system *(pages 6–7)*.

Water purity
If the water comes from a utility company, it is tested regularly to ensure it is safe to drink. If you have a private well, testing for purity is your responsibility. If your water tastes bad or produces stains, running the main supply line through a water softener and/or a water filter may help.

Water meter
If your water bill is the same from month to month, you probably have unmetered water. If you have a water meter, the bill reflects how much water enters your house. A water meter may be found inside the house, or it may be in the Buffalo box outside.

Water heater
Near the water heater, one pipe branches off to supply cold water throughout the house, and another enters a gas or electric water heater, which typically holds and heats 30 to 50 gallons of water. A supply pipe exits the heater to deliver hot water throughout the house. If you often run out of hot water while bathing, consider buying a water heater with a larger capacity.

Supply pipes
Supply pipes run in pairs throughout the house. Vertical pipes are called risers.

Supply pipes may be copper, galvanized steel, or plastic. Galvanized steel pipes rust and corrode in time, causing leaks that lower water pressure. Plastic PVC supply pipes have been banned by most communities for interior use because the joints may come loose in time. Newer plastic pipes, made of rigid CPVC or flexible polyethylene (PE), are more reliable and are permitted in many areas. Copper is the material of choice in most areas. It is long-lasting and its smooth surface does not collect deposits that slow the flow of water. A properly soldered joint, using lead-free solder, is as strong as the pipe itself.

A nail or screw can easily pierce a copper or plastic supply pipe, so plumbing codes prescribe measures to keep supply pipes out of harm's way. Pipes within walls should be placed in the center of studs so that nails cannot reach them. Protective metal plates may also be required.

Pipe sizes and water pressure
The larger a pipe's inside diameter, the greater the water pressure. If water pressure is too low, the problem may be the supply pipes.

The pipe bringing water into a house is typically 1 inch or 1¼ inches inside diameter. Soon after entering the house, the size narrows to ¾ inch. Pipes that carry water from room to room may be either ¾ or ½ inch; the larger size is preferable. Pipes that supply water to specific fixtures are usually ½ inch to the stop, then ¼ inch.

A bathtub access panel

Bathtub plumbing is complicated, so many homes have an access panel to allow you to reach it. To find an access panel, look in the adjacent room or closet, on the wall directly behind the tub faucet.

Locating supply lines

Near the water heater, supply lines branch into cold and hot pipes— an excellent place to start tracing your supply system. Most water heaters stamp "hot" and "cold" on the top of the metal housing.

Some lines reduce in dimension along their run. Here a pipe steps down in size from ¾ inch to ½ inch.

HOUSEHOLD SUPPLY SYSTEM

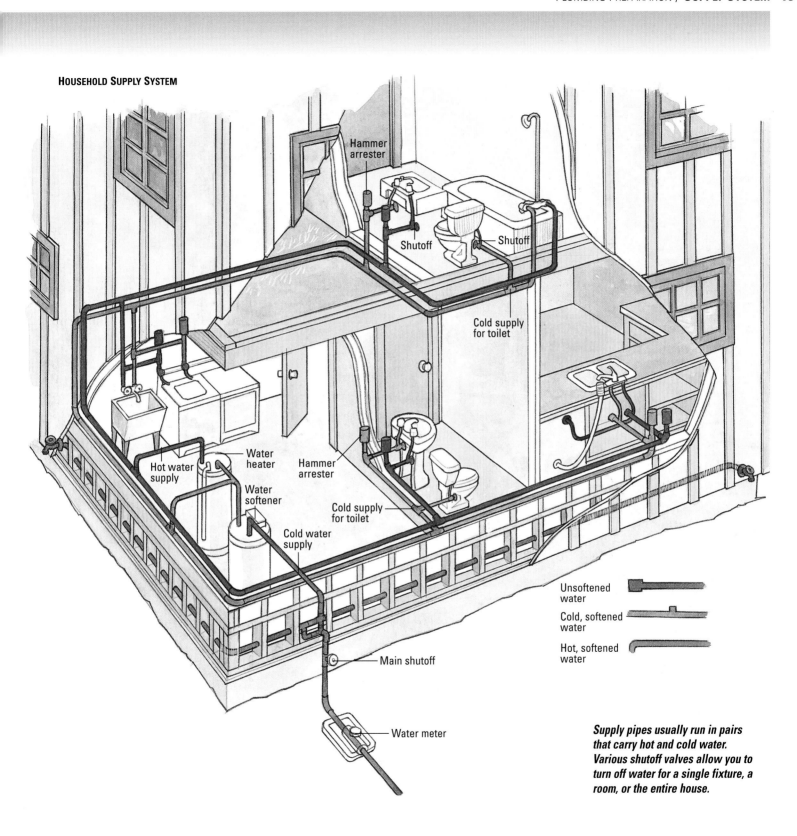

Hammer
arrester

Shutoff

Shutoff

Cold supply
for toilet

Hot water
supply

Water
heater

Hammer
arrester

Water
softener

Cold supply
for toilet

Cold water
supply

Unsoftened
water

Cold, softened
water

Hot, softened
water

Main shutoff

Water meter

*Supply pipes usually run in pairs
that carry hot and cold water.
Various shutoff valves allow you to
turn off water for a single fixture, a
room, or the entire house.*

PIPES AND FITTINGS

When making repairs or installing new fixtures, you'll need to know the pipe type and size. Newer homes usually have plastic drainpipes and copper supply pipes; a pre-1950 home may have cast-iron drain and galvanized steel supply pipes.

Plastic

Plastic pipe is inexpensive and easy to work with, making it popular among installers. Joints are glued together using a primer to clean and prepare the surface and a cement made for the particular type of plastic.

White or cream-colored **PVC (polyvinyl chloride)** pipe is the most common choice for drainpipes. It's strong, lasts nearly forever, and is nearly impervious to chemicals. PVC is sometimes used for supply pipes, but codes in most communities no longer allow it for hot water supply lines because heat causes it to shrink, weakening joints. Stamped printing on the pipe tells you the pipe's size and schedule—its strength rating. Schedule 40 is considered strong enough for most residential purposes.

CPVC (chlorinated polyvinyl chloride) pipe has the strength of PVC and is also heat-resistant, so many codes allow its use for interior supply lines.

Black **ABS (acrylonitrile-butadiene-styrene)** drainpipe was the first plastic pipe to be used in homes. Many localities no longer permit its use; PVC is considered a superior material.

Flexible **PE (polyethylene)** supply pipe is the newest type of plastic pipe. Many codes restrict its use.

Copper

Copper pipe is long-lasting and resists corrosion, making it ideal for supply pipes. It is more expensive than plastic but still reasonably priced.

Rigid copper pipe comes in three thicknesses. The thinnest, rated "M," is usually considered strong enough for most residential purposes. Thicker pipes, rated "L" or "K," are used outdoors. Rigid copper pipe is joined to fittings by sweating, soldering the pieces together using a propane torch. A well-soldered joint is wiped smooth. If there is a visible drip of solder, the joint may not be strong.

Flexible copper tubing is often used to supply a dishwasher or other appliance. Small-diameter flexible copper is commonly used as a supply for an ice maker. The

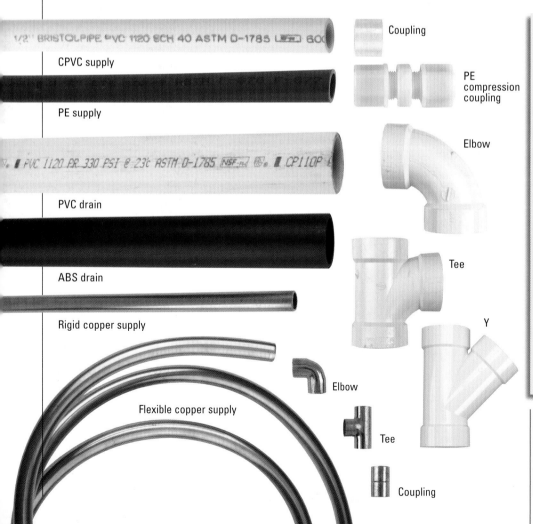

CPVC supply

PE supply

PVC drain

ABS drain

Rigid copper supply

Flexible copper supply

Coupling

PE compression coupling

Elbow

Tee

Y

Elbow

Tee

Coupling

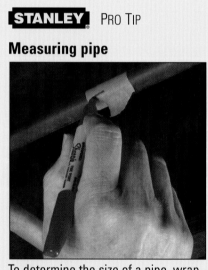

STANLEY PRO TIP

Measuring pipe

To determine the size of a pipe, wrap a piece of tape or a strip of paper—something that will not stretch—around it. Make a mark to indicate the outside circumference of the pipe. Consult the chart opposite to find the inside diameter of the pipe.

Standard diameters

Supply pipes usually have an inside diameter of ½ inch, ¾ inch, or 1 inch. Drainpipe generally ranges in size from 1½ inches to 4 inches.

tubing is easily bent to make fairly tight turns. If it gets kinked, however, there's no way to fix it; the piece must be replaced. It is joined to fittings and valves using compression fittings *(page 100)*.

Steel

Many older homes have **galvanized steel pipes** for supply lines, and sometimes for branch drain lines as well. It has a dull gray color. Galvanized pipe is strong—a nail has a hard time piercing it—but its useful life is only 50 years or so. Joints develop rust and, more importantly, the insides become clogged with mineral deposits, causing reduced water flow. Galvanized drainpipe rarely gets clogged enough to stop water from flowing, but the joints may rust and leak.

Black steel pipe is used for gas lines only. It should not be used for water supply because it rusts more quickly than galvanized steel. (An exception: In some areas, black steel is used for water supply lines leading into a boiler that heats the house.) Yellow-coated black pipe is used for underground gas lines.

Steel pipe is joined to fittings by first wrapping the threads with white pipe-thread tape (yellow for gas pipes) or covering them with pipe dope (which may be gray, white, or yellow), then tightening. The joints must be very tight so they cannot be loosened without a long pipe wrench. Inadequately tightened joints will leak eventually.

Cast iron

Used only for drain lines and vents, **cast-iron pipe** is heavy and strong. Many people prefer cast iron to plastic drainpipe because cast iron deadens the sound of running water, while plastic seems to amplify it.

Cast iron often lasts over a hundred years. However, it's not unusual for one or two sections to rust through while the rest of the pipe remains in good shape.

Traditionally, cast-iron pipe is joined together by first stuffing oakum (a loose rope of greasy fiber) into the joint, then pouring in molten lead. Newer "no-hub" fittings use a neoprene sleeve and pipe clamps to join pipes together.

Fittings

Whenever pipe turns a corner or branches off, a fitting is required. **Elbows** (or "els") make 90- or 45-degree turns. **Tees** and **Ys** allow for pipes to branch off. **Couplings** join two pipes together.

PIPE SIZES

Material	Outside Circumference	Inside Diameter
Copper	2"	1/2"
	2¾"	3/4"
	3½"	1"
Steel (galvanized or black)	2"	3/8"
	2⅜"	1/2"
	3⅛"	3/4"
	4"	1"
	4¾"	1¼"
	5½"	1½"
	7"	2"
Plastic (PVC, CPVC, or ABS)	2¾"	1/2"
	3½"	3/4"
	4¼"	1"
	5⅛"	1¼"
	6"	1½"
	7½"	2"
	10½"	3"
	14"	4"
Cast Iron	7"	2"
	10⅛"	3"
	13⅜"	4"

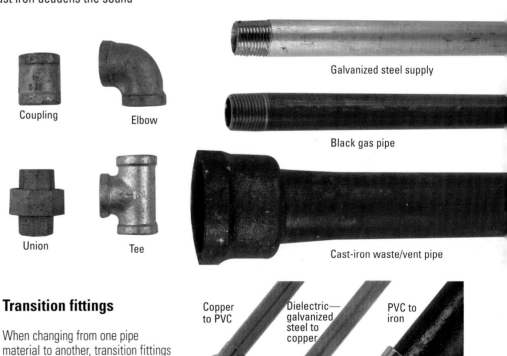

Coupling

Elbow

Union

Tee

Galvanized steel supply

Black gas pipe

Cast-iron waste/vent pipe

Transition fittings

When changing from one pipe material to another, transition fittings are used. A steel-to-copper transition will corrode quickly unless a dielectric fitting is used—it has a plastic washer that separates the metals. Other transition fittings join copper to plastic, plastic to steel, and plastic to cast iron.

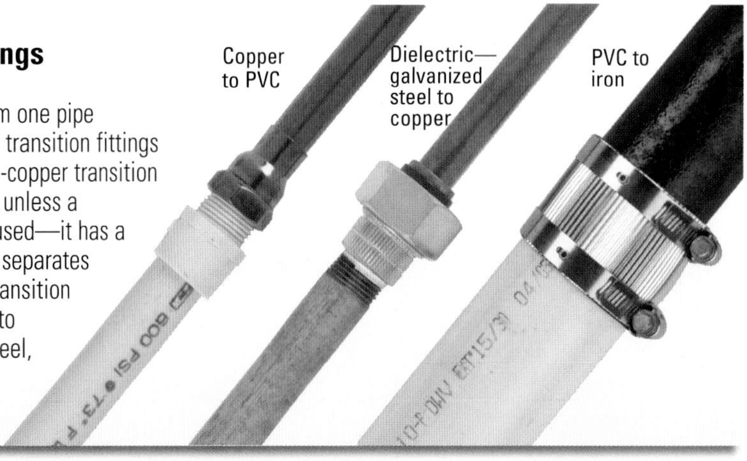

Copper to PVC

Dielectric— galvanized steel to copper

PVC to iron

COMMON PLUMBING SYSTEM PROBLEMS

Most of the pipes in a home are hidden behind walls. But there is usually enough exposed plumbing to permit an inspection, and most common problems can be spotted by a nonprofessional. If you encounter a possible problem that you do not understand, call in a professional for an evaluation.

Mapping the pipes

If you're lucky, you will have architectural drawings of your home that diagram where all the pipes go. If not, do a bit of sleuthing and make some rough drawings that map your system so you can quickly find pipes when you need to make repairs or new installations.

The drawings on *pages 11 and 13* give a general idea of how most systems are put together. First, locate the main stack and any secondary stack; all the drain lines will tie into these. Often the wall with the main stack—called a plumbing wall—is thicker than other walls to accommodate the hefty drainpipes.

Look for access panels *(page 12),* which allow you a peek at the innards of the system. If no access panel exists behind a tub, consider installing one. You can buy a ready-made panel at a home center.

From a basement or crawlspace, you may be able to look up and see where pipes run. When traveling through a wall of a room that has no plumbing fixtures, vertical pipes almost always travel straight up.

To map the supply pipes, start at the shutoff, then find where they branch off near the water heater.

Checking for lead

Pipe that is a dull gray color and flexible enough to make tight bends may be made of lead. If you can easily dig into it with a knife, it's definitely lead. Lead poisoning is a serious matter: Have lead pipe replaced.

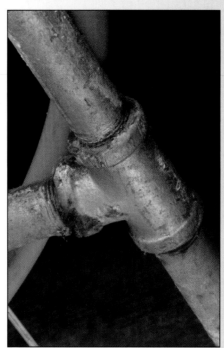

A rusted joint in a galvanized pipe is worth watching. The joint may remain leak-free for decades, or it may start to drip tomorrow. Check it regularly.

Exposed copper and plastic pipe can be cracked or dented if subjected to misuse or abuse. If children are tempted to hang on pipes, cover them up. **Do not hang objects from pipes.**

STANLEY PRO TIP: **When pipes gurgle, hammer, and sloosh**

If you hear a gurgling sound in the wall when water drains out of a sink, a vent pipe may be clogged. Check the roof; it's not unheard of for a roofer to partially or completely cover up a vent. Run an auger through the vent pipes, either going down from the roof or up from the room below.

If water gurgles when the dishwasher drains, check the drain hose. It should either run through an air gap—a cylindrical device that mounts to the sink—or in a loop that rises at one point up as high as possible, just under the sink.

If water makes a banging noise when you quickly turn a faucet on or off, your pipes have "water hammer." The solution is to install a water-hammer arrester, like the tub/shower installation shown at right. An arrester can be retrofitted where lines are accessible *(page 113).*

Water hammer arrester

Tape repairs are a temporary fix at best. If a trap has been repaired with tape, expect that it will leak soon. If one part of the trap is corroded, other parts probably are as well, so replace the entire trap *(pages 24–25)*.

Structural damage results when plumbers hack away at joists and other framing members to install drainpipes. If the floor or ceiling sags near plumbing, you may need to shore up the framing.

Solder drips often indicate a weak joint. Or worse, lead solder may have been used to join older copper pipe. If you can easily scrape the solder with a knife, it may be lead. Call in a professional for evaluation.

WHAT IF…
You have low water pressure?

If you have low water pressure, open a hose bib or other faucet located near the point where water enters the house. If the pressure there seems low, contact your water supplier. If pressure is strong at the point of entry but weak elsewhere, try clearing aerators and showerheads *(pages 20–21)*.

If the problem is more general, some of your supply pipes may be undersized. If the pipes are galvanized, chances are they are partially clogged with mineral deposits or rust. Replacing some horizontal pipes may increase the pressure.

One technique plumbers use to increase water pressure is to run water backward through the pipes, from an upper-story faucet down to the basement. Look for a plumbing contractor who specializes in clearing old galvanized supply pipes.

Catch basin

People tend to pour grease down kitchen sinks. In time, doing so can clog drain lines. In many older homes, the kitchen sink has its own stack and the drain line runs outside to a catch basin— a container that traps grease in one of its chambers. Once in a great while, you must remove the grease from the catch basin.

A catch basin typically is located in the backyard and has a large metal cover. In many cases, however, the catch basin has been bypassed and is no longer in use.

DEALING WITH CLOGGED PIPES

If a drain runs sluggishly or is stopped up, the plumbing is probably fine, though it's likely clogged with grease, soap, hair, or a small object. If you have children, the culprit may be a small toy.

Preventive measures

Always use the toilet, not the sink, to dispose of semisolid waste. However, even a toilet cannot handle large objects: Sanitary napkins, tampons, and big wads of toilet paper can clog it.

Equip sinks and tubs with strainers, and regularly clear away hair and gunk.

Food that has been ground up in a garbage disposer can form a thick paste, especially if grease is part of the mix. Keep grease out of the sink whenever possible. Use cold water when running the disposer, then run hot water for a few seconds to clear the trap.

Diagnosing and unclogging

If only one fixture is sluggish or stopped up, the clog is probably in the fixture's trap or in the branch drain line. If more than one fixture is affected, the problem is farther down the line—most likely in a drainpipe or even the stack. If all the fixtures on the first floor are clogged, the main drain may need to be augered— a job for professionals.

This chapter describes basic unclogging methods, beginning with the simplest. Start by plunging. If that doesn't work, move on to dismantling a trap and possibly replacing the trap. If the problem is farther down the line, use an auger.

Bathtubs, bathroom drains, and kitchen strainers all call for special solutions, described on *pages 30–35.*

For low water pressure in a faucet or showerhead, *pages 20–21* show how to increase the flow.

Working safely

Chances are you will get splashed while unclogging a drain. If drain cleaner has been poured down the drain, unclogging it can be dangerous (see box opposite). When working with drain cleaner, wear plastic gloves, long sleeves, and safety goggles. Cover the work area with an old rug or a drop cloth before starting work.

CHAPTER PREVIEW

Clogged and sluggish pipes can usually be cleared using simple techniques and a few tools.

Clearing aerators and showerheads
page 20

Clearing clogs by plunging
page 22

Dismantling a trap
page 24

Augering sinks, tubs, or toilets
page 26

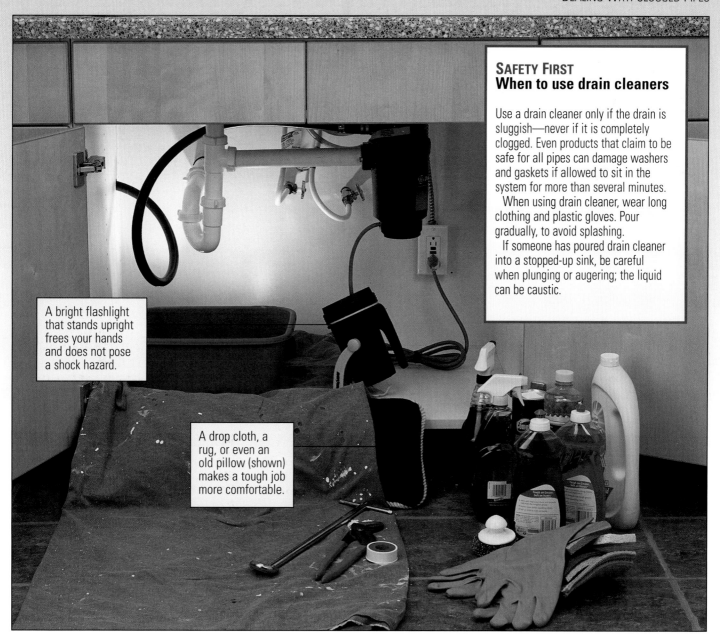

SAFETY FIRST
When to use drain cleaners

Use a drain cleaner only if the drain is sluggish—never if it is completely clogged. Even products that claim to be safe for all pipes can damage washers and gaskets if allowed to sit in the system for more than several minutes.

When using drain cleaner, wear long clothing and plastic gloves. Pour gradually, to avoid splashing.

If someone has poured drain cleaner into a stopped-up sink, be careful when plunging or augering; the liquid can be caustic.

A bright flashlight that stands upright frees your hands and does not pose a shock hazard.

A drop cloth, a rug, or even an old pillow (shown) makes a tough job more comfortable.

Working under a sink can be downright miserable. Make the work site as comfortable as possible by adding a drop cloth, a rug, and even an old pillow, especially where the edge of the cabinet can dig into your back. Place tools so they are easily reached, and set up a flashlight.

Heavy augering
page 28

Tub and shower drain repairs
page 30

Bathroom sink drain
page 32

Kitchen basket strainer
page 34

CLEARING AERATORS AND SHOWERHEADS

An aerator screws onto the end of a faucet. It typically has two screens through which water passes, creating a mixture of water and air that produces a smooth flow and minimizes splash.

Tiny particles caught in an aerator's screens reduce the water flow. The solution is usually simple: Just unscrew and take apart the aerator, flush the particles out of the screens, reassemble, and screw it back on.

If aerators clog regularly, your water system may be at fault. If your home has old galvanized steel pipes, particles are probably flaking off the inside of the pipes *(page 17)* and may need to be flushed. If your home has copper supply pipes, the problem may be that the water delivered by the utility company is impure; try installing a water filter.

If water flows slowly into a washing machine, shut off the stop valves and unscrew the hoses. You'll find a screen at the end of the hose; if it is stopped up with particles, clean it out.

PRESTART CHECKLIST

☐ **TIME**
Just a few minutes to clean out an aerator or showerhead. If mineral deposits are severe, soak the parts overnight.

☐ **TOOLS**
Groove-joint pliers, screwdriver, old toothbrush, straight pin

☐ **SKILLS**
No special skills needed

☐ **PREP**
Cover the sink or shower drain so small parts can't accidentally slip down it.

☐ **MATERIALS**
Vinegar, lime-deposit cleaner

Aerators

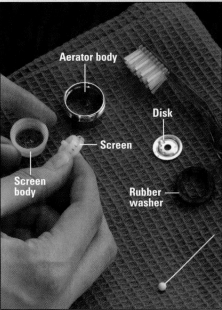

1 You may be able to unscrew an aerator with your fingers. If not, wrap masking tape around the aerator to protect it from scratching, and unscrew it with groove-joint pliers. Turn the faucet on and off several times to flush out any additional debris.

2 Disassemble the aerator with your fingers or use a small screwdriver. Note how the pieces go together. If the aerator is damaged, buy a replacement. Clean the screens with a toothbrush and pin, and rinse. If the minerals are caked on, soak them in vinegar overnight and clean again.

AERATOR TYPES

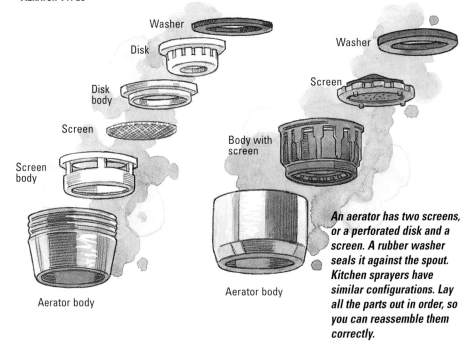

An aerator has two screens, or a perforated disk and a screen. A rubber washer seals it against the spout. Kitchen sprayers have similar configurations. Lay all the parts out in order, so you can reassemble them correctly.

Showerheads

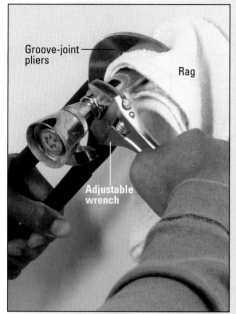

Groove-joint pliers

Rag

Adjustable wrench

1 Unscrew the showerhead collar with an adjustable wrench. If the shower arm turns while you are doing this, grip it with groove-joint pliers while you unscrew the showerhead. Wrap a cloth around the shower arm to keep from damaging it.

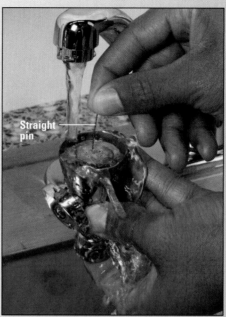

Straight pin

2 Run water backward through the showerhead and poke the spray outlets with a pin or brush to flush out the debris.

3 If the debris does not flush out easily, soak the showerhead overnight in a solution of vinegar and lime-deposit cleaner and try again. You may need to disassemble the showerhead and clean all the parts individually. If the showerhead is damaged, buy a new one.

TWO TYPES OF SHOWERHEADS

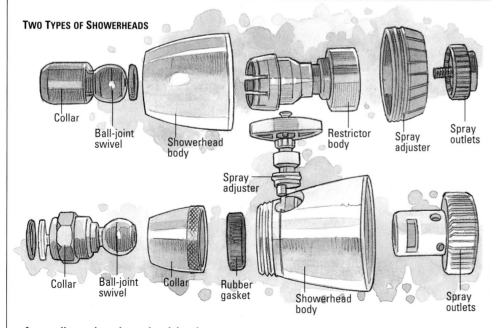

Collar

Ball-joint swivel

Showerhead body

Spray adjuster

Restrictor body

Spray adjuster

Spray outlets

Collar

Ball-joint swivel

Collar

Rubber gasket

Showerhead body

Spray outlets

As you dismantle a showerhead, lay the parts out in order so you can easily reassemble them later.

STANLEY PRO TIP

Check the flow restrictor

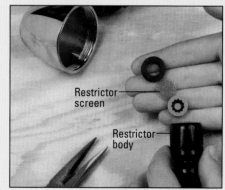

Restrictor screen

Restrictor body

To conserve water, many newer showerheads have built-in flow restrictors. If the water pressure in the shower is low, check to see if the restrictor is clogged with mineral deposits. Dismantle the restrictor and soak its parts overnight in a bowl of lime-deposit cleaner.

CLEARING CLOGS BY PLUNGING

If a sink or tub is clogged, try running hot water through it. Check the strainer (if there is one) and clean out any hair or debris that may have collected. If water still drains slowly, the next step is plunging.

To use a flanged plunger on a sink or tub, fold the flange into the body of the plunger. For small sinks, you may find that a regular plunger works best.

Plunging works in two ways: by pushing a clog through to the stack, and by pulling debris back up into the sink.

For tough jobs, you may want to try a pressure-type plunger, which looks a bit like an accordion *(page 8)*. It generates greater pressure than a standard plunger.

Before plunging, make sure the water has only one exit point—through the drain. Plug overflow holes and clamp connecting hoses before you begin.

Sometimes plunging works easily, with little mess. Other times, water sprays all over the place. Be prepared to wipe up substantial amounts of water.

PRESTART CHECKLIST

☐ **TIME**
About half an hour to prepare and plunge a sink, tub, or toilet

☐ **TOOLS**
Regular, flanged, or pressure-type plunger

☐ **SKILLS**
No special skills needed

☐ **PREP**
Block any alternate passageways through which plunged water may flow.

☐ **MATERIALS**
No special materials needed

1 If a drain is sluggish, wait for most of the water to drain out. If the drain is clogged, bail out the water. For best results, there should be about 2 inches of standing water in the sink—just enough to cover the plunger.

2 Often hair and gunk caught on the stopper is the cause of the clog. Remove the stopper and clean it off. (If the stopper does not pull out easily, see *page 32*.) If the sink still does not drain readily, the real clog is farther down the line.

WHAT IF...
A double-drain sink is clogged?

Before plunging a kitchen drain connected to a dishwasher, tightly clamp the drain hose (inset), usually attached to a garbage disposer under the sink. If the sink has two bowls, have a helper block one drain with a second plunger while you plunge the other.

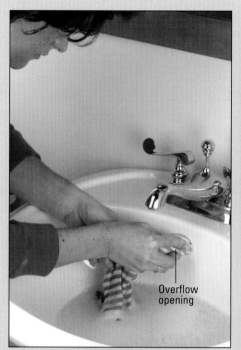

Overflow opening

Non-flanged plunger

Pull out debris.

3 Stuff a wet rag into the overflow opening so water cannot spurt through it as you use the plunger. A helper may need to hold the rag in place as you plunge.

4 Make sure the plunger forms a tight seal around the drain hole. Work the plunger with a steady, firm, up-and-down motion. You'll feel the water pushing and pulling through the drain. If the clog does not clear immediately, don't give up. Make at least several attempts.

5 If the water suddenly drains out, the clog has passed out of the drainpipe and into the stack, or the plunger has sucked debris back into the sink. If the drain remains clogged after numerous attempts at plunging, move on to dismantling the trap *(pages 24–25)*.

Plunging a tub

Stuff overflow opening with a rag.

Before plunging a bathtub, remove the drain assembly *(pages 30–31)* and stop the overflow hole with a wet rag. Remove the strainer and bail or add water until there is just enough water to cover the plunger.

Plunging a toilet

Flange

To plunge a toilet, use a flanged plunger with the flange pulled out. Fit the flange into the drain hole, seat the body of the plunger firmly around the hole, and push and pull vigorously.

STANLEY PRO TIP

Pushing through with water pressure

Use an expansion nozzle (also called a balloon or blow bag) to blast a blockage through to the stack. Attach the nozzle to a garden hose, insert it into the drain, and turn on the hose. The nozzle will expand to seal around the drain. Pressure builds until a burst of water is released to clear the clog. **Check your local codes to make sure the use of this tool is allowed in your area.**

DISMANTLING A TRAP

A trap not only seals out gases *(page 10)*, it also provides a bottleneck that prevents clogs from traveling farther down the line. That's why most clogs are found in a trap bend.

To clear a clog, dismantle the trap and clean it out. You'll probably need to replace some rubber washers—they get brittle with age. It's not unusual to find that the entire trap needs replacing. If even one component is leaky, replace the entire trap rather than a single piece—one worn component is likely to mean wear in others. Less expensive chrome-plated traps are notoriously short-lived. They may look OK on the outside, but squeeze the bottom of the bend with your fingers. If you feel it give, even slightly, the metal is corroded. For durability, buy a plastic trap or a chrome-plated trap that is made of heavy-gauge brass.

Bathroom traps are 1¼ inches in diameter; kitchen drains are 1½ inches.

PRESTART CHECKLIST

☐ **TIME**
About an hour to dismantle and reinstall a trap

☐ **TOOLS**
Groove-joint pliers, screwdriver, toothbrush, hacksaw, sandpaper

☐ **SKILLS**
Dismantling and connecting parts with washers and nuts

☐ **PREP**
Prepare a comfortable work site *(page 19)* and have a bucket or dishpan and a drop cloth in place.

☐ **MATERIALS**
Washers, pipe tape, perhaps a new trap

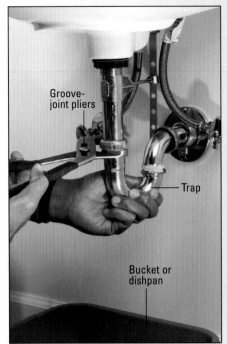

Groove-joint pliers

Trap

Bucket or dishpan

1 Place a bucket under the trap. Loosen the nut on each side of the curved piece with groove-joint pliers. Slide the nuts out of the way and pull the curved piece off.

2 Use a toothbrush to remove hair and other debris that has collected in the trap. If the trap is in good shape, replace the washers and reassemble it. If any parts are damaged, install a new trap (Steps 3–5).

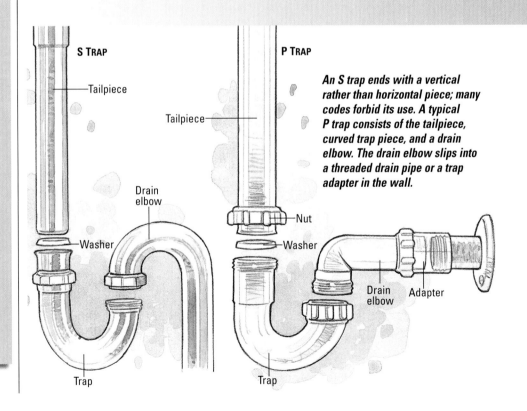

S TRAP

Tailpiece

Drain elbow

Washer

Trap

P TRAP

Tailpiece

Nut

Washer

Drain elbow

Adapter

Trap

An S trap ends with a vertical rather than horizontal piece; many codes forbid its use. A typical P trap consists of the tailpiece, curved trap piece, and a drain elbow. The drain elbow slips into a threaded drain pipe or a trap adapter in the wall.

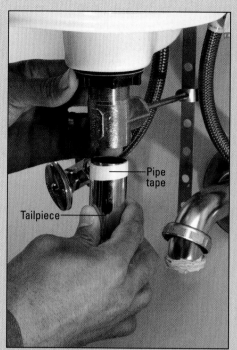

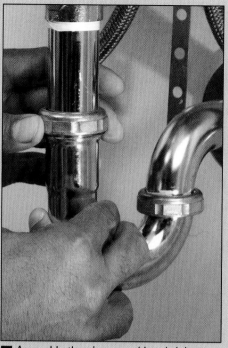

3 Take the old parts to a home center or hardware store to find replacements. Make sure the new pieces will fit exactly; you may need to cut the tailpiece or drain elbow. Begin assembly by wrapping pipe tape clockwise around the threads of a tailpiece, and screw it onto the drain body.

4 With the tailpiece installed, dry-fit all the pieces to make sure they join together with ease. If you have to force a connection, it may leak. For each joint, slide on the nut, then the washer.

5 Assemble the pieces and hand-tighten all the nuts. Then go back and tighten the nuts with groove-joint pliers. To test the drain for leaks, stop up the sink, fill it with water, and open the stopper. Watch carefully for any leaks as the water flows through. Tighten joints where necessary.

CUT THE TAILPIECE
Cutting trap components

To cut a chrome-plated trap piece, place it in a miter box and cut with a hacksaw. To avoid denting the pipe, exert gentle pressure as you cut. After cutting, remove any burrs with sandpaper.

STANLEY PRO TIP

Plastic vs. metal traps

Metal usually is associated with durability, but in the case of sink traps, plastic is the long-lasting choice. Usually you can replace a chrome trap with a plastic one; just make sure it's the right size for the sink and the wall pipe. If appearance is important, choose a chrome-plated brass trap.

Trap with a cleanout plug

Some heavy-duty traps are equipped with a cleanout, a plug that can be removed. Place a bucket under the trap, unscrew the plug, and let the water run out. Reach inside with an auger to remove debris.

AUGERING SINKS, TUBS, OR TOILETS

An inexpensive hand-crank drum auger clears most household clogs. It consists of a snakelike cable made of metal, with a widened tip that grabs or pushes debris. Power-operated augers work quicker but are a bit dangerous; if the clog is solid, a fast-turning auger is likely to get stuck so tightly you cannot extract it.

Before use, check that the tip of the auger is in good shape. If it is broken or has come unwound, buy a new auger.

You may choose to run an auger through the sink and into the trap, rather than dismantling the trap. However, before doing so on a bathroom sink, you'll need to remove the pivot rod *(page 32)*. It's usually not possible to auger a kitchen sink, because of the garbage disposer and because the drain assembly for a double-bowl sink has too many turns.

PRESTART CHECKLIST

☐ **TIME**
About 2 hours to dismantle a trap and auger a branch line

☐ **TOOLS**
Groove-joint pliers, hand-crank auger

☐ **SKILLS**
Dismantling and reinstalling a trap

☐ **PREP**
Make the work site comfortable; place a bucket under the trap to catch spilled water.

☐ **MATERIALS**
Replacement washers for the trap

1 Dismantle the trap. You can run an auger through the trap arm, but it's easier to auger with the trap arm removed.

2 Loosen the auger setscrew and pull out about a foot of the cable. Push the cable through the pipe until it stops. You've probably run into a bend in the pipe, rather than the obstruction.

WHAT IF...
You must auger a tub?

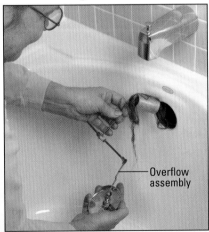

1 To auger a bathtub, first check to see whether there is a drum trap in the bathroom *(page 29)*. If so, auger from there. Otherwise remove the overflow assembly *(pages 30–31)*.

2 Run the auger down through the overflow, using the techniques shown above.

3 Pull out enough cable so the setscrew is several inches from the point of entry. Tighten the setscrew and crank clockwise until the cable moves forward.

4 Loosen the setscrew, push forward as far as the cable will go, tighten the setscrew again, and crank. Repeat the process until you reach an obstruction. If you feel the clog give way, you may have pushed it through. Pull out the auger and run water to test.

5 The auger may grab rather than push the obstruction. If so, pull out the auger, clean away any hair and gunk, and push the auger in again to remove more of the obstruction.

TOILET AUGER

A toilet auger has a rubber sleeve to protect the porcelain from scratches. It's just the right length and shape to get at clogs inside and just beyond a toilet.

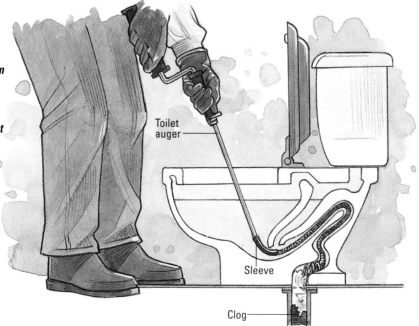

Toilet auger

Sleeve

Clog

WHAT IF...
The auger gets stuck?

If you suspect that an auger is in danger of getting stuck, pull it out rather than pushing and turning further. It may take four or five attempts before the clog is removed or pushed through.

If an auger does get stuck, tighten the setscrew and turn the crank counterclockwise. This usually frees it. If that doesn't work, push and pull rapidly back and forth.

It may take some time, but these measures almost always work. If the auger will not come loose after repeated tries, call a professional plumber for help.

HEAVY AUGERING

If more than one fixture is stopped up, or if you cannot clear a clog by plunging or augering from the trap location, it may be time to auger branch drain lines or a stack or a main drain.

If a drainpipe is exposed, you may be able to locate the clog by tapping on the pipe with a piece of wood. You've found the clog when you hear a dull thud instead of a hollow ring. Then find the nearest cleanout to auger out the obstruction.

To auger branch lines and a stack, you may want to rent or buy a handheld power auger; a hand-crank drum auger may not be powerful enough. If you need to auger a main drain, consider hiring a pro or renting a motorized auger. Have a salesperson show you how to use it.

PRESTART CHECKLIST

☐ **TIME**
1 or 2 hours to auger a branch drain line

☐ **TOOLS**
Hand-crank or power auger, groove-joint pliers, pipe wrench, or adjustable wrench

☐ **SKILLS**
Dismantling a cleanout or trap cover, running an auger through pipes

☐ **PREP**
Position a bucket and drop cloth to catch and wipe up spills.

☐ **MATERIALS**
Replacement cover for a drain trap, pipe tape to replace a cleanout plug

Using a cleanout

Hand-crank auger

1 Locate a cleanout on the drain line that is clogged *(page 11)*. The pipe may be filled with dirty water that will pour out when you open the plug, so position a bucket to catch the water. Using an adjustable wrench or groove-joint pliers, remove the cleanout plug.

2 Run a hand-crank auger through the drainpipe, using the techniques shown on *pages 26–27*.

WHAT IF...
You have a brass plug?

If a cast-iron pipe has a brass cleanout plug, remove it with an adjustable wrench. After augering, wrap its threads with pipe tape before reinstalling. If the plug is damaged, install an expandable rubber plug similar to the one shown for a drum trap *(page 29)*.

AUGERING FROM THE ROOF

Auger

Vent stack

The easiest way to auger a stack is from the roof, pushing down; that way, you have gravity on your side. Be sure to establish firm footholds before working on a roof.

Drum trap

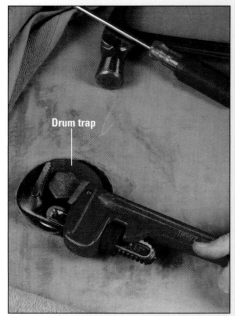

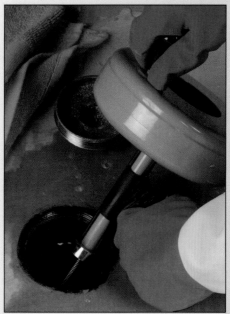

1 Many older homes have a drum trap located on the bathroom floor. If the cover is too corroded to be removed with an adjustable wrench, use a hammer and large screwdriver to force it loose.

2 If the trap itself contains the clog, dig the gunk out and replace the cover. Otherwise determine where the lines run (see illustration below) and run an auger through a line that goes to the tub, to the sink, or to the stack.

3 If you damaged the cover when removing it, install a replacement cover with a rubber seal that expands as you tighten a wing nut. It will seal the drum trap tight and will make it easier to open next time you have to auger.

Drum traps

Some drum traps have two covers with a trap between them; most clogs will be located in the trap.

An older type of drum trap is cylindrical. Lines coming in from a tub and/or sink enter the drum at a point that is lower than the connection for the drain line leading out to the stack.

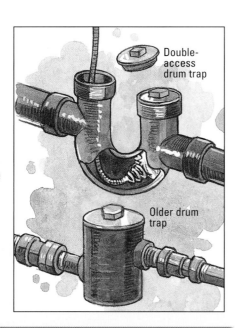

Double-access drum trap

Older drum trap

Hand-held power auger

Some crank augers have a shaft that fits the chuck of a power drill, as well as a hand crank. Use a variable-speed drill only—a single-speed drill turns too fast, which can jam the auger in the pipe.

TUB AND SHOWER DRAIN REPAIRS

A bathtub overflow drain assembly includes a stopper, which allows the tub to fill, and an overflow hole, which keeps water from overfilling the tub. If water drains slowly, a debris-clogged drain assembly may be the culprit. If the the stopper does not seal completely, you may need to adjust the assembly.

Drain types
There are three basic types of bathtub drain assemblies:

A plunger assembly has a brass cylinder (or plunger) that slides up and down through the brass overflow pipe to open or close the drain.

A pop-up drain has a rocker arm that pivots like a seesaw to raise or lower the stopper. A trip lever attached to an adjustable rod with a spring at the end controls the rocker arm.

An overflow unit equipped with a lift-and-drain or push-down stopper has no interior mechanism—just lift up or depress the stopper with your hand or foot.

PRESTART CHECKLIST

☐ **TIME**
About an hour to remove, adjust, and reinstall a drain assembly

☐ **TOOLS**
Screwdriver, pliers, toothbrush

☐ **SKILLS**
Working carefully with small parts

☐ **PREP**
Clean out the tub and spread out a towel on which you can lay the parts.

☐ **MATERIALS**
Heatproof plumber's grease

Plunger type assembly

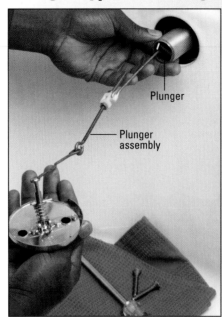

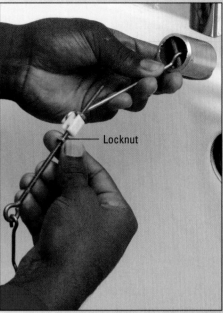

1 Remove the screws that hold the upper cover plate. Pull the entire assembly—cover plate, linkage, and plunger—up and out. It will slide out in one piece. Clean away any debris with a toothbrush. Brush the plunger with heatproof plumber's grease before reinstalling it.

2 If the stopper does not completely stop water from draining, adjust the linkage. Loosen the locknut, twist the rod so the plunger moves downward ⅛ inch or so, and retighten the locknut. Feed the entire assembly back in and test; you may need to make additional adjustments.

BATHTUB WASTE AND OVERFLOW ASSEMBLIES

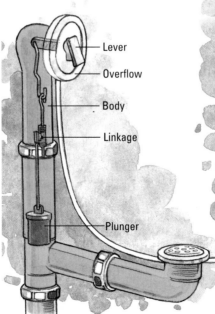

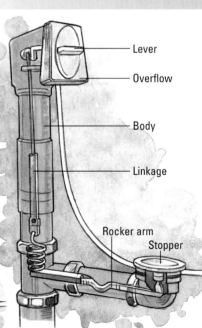

If a bathtub drain is controlled by a lever at the overflow hole, it is either a plunger type (left) or a pop-up (rocker-arm) type (above).

Pop-up (rocker-arm) type assembly

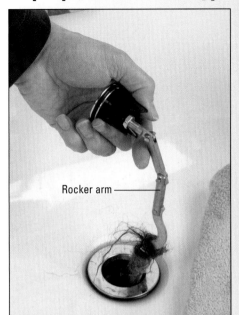

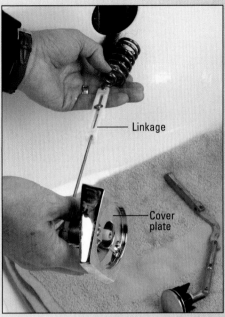

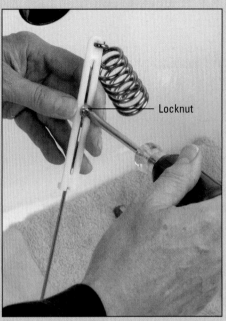

Rocker arm

Linkage

Cover plate

Locknut

1 If the tub has a pop-up assembly, flip the trip lever up to raise the stopper. Gently pull the stopper and the rocker arm up and out of the tub. Clean away any debris.

2 Remove the cover plate screws and pull out the cover plate with the linkage connected to it. Clean away any hair and other debris that might be attached to the linkage.

3 If the stopper does not seal completely, loosen the locknut and twist the threaded rod so it rises up about ⅛ inch. Tighten the locknut. Reinstall and test.

STANLEY PRO TIP

Salvage the assembly

Replacing an entire drain assembly is difficult. Fortunately most pop-up and rocker-arm drains are made of long-lasting brass, so they can be cleaned and reused for many years.

If the linkage is tangled with hair or other waste matter, there may be more in the drain. Plunge or auger the drain before reinstalling the assembly.

If an assembly is caked with mineral deposits, it cannot operate smoothly. Soak the parts overnight in a small tub filled with a mixture of lime-deposit cleaner and vinegar.

Lift-and-drain tub stoppers

The simplest and least expensive drain assemblies consist of only one mechanism: a stopper that you can operate with your hand, or even your toe. The body of this assembly is usually plastic.

One type is operated simply by pushing down to either open or close the stopper. With another type, you pull up and twist to open the stopper.

If one of this type of stoppers fails to seal, replace the rubber O-ring.

If the stopper is damaged, it's easy to replace. Simply unscrew it with a pair of pliers. When screwing the new one in, press down gently, because the plastic fitting that you are screwing into may not be solidly attached.

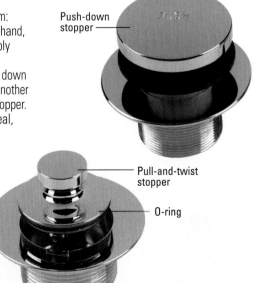

Push-down stopper

Pull-and-twist stopper

O-ring

BATHROOM SINK DRAIN

The pop-up assembly on a bathroom drain has several moving parts that wear out over time. If the unit is made of thin metal or plastic that is easily bent or broken, repairs may not last; consider buying a new faucet and drain assembly.

Troubleshooting

■ If a stopper is loose and won't stay open, tighten the pivot ball retaining nut.

■ If a stopper is difficult to raise, loosen the pivot ball retaining nut. If that doesn't work, remove the pivot rod, clean out the opening in the drain body, and replace worn gaskets or washers.

■ If the stopper does not seat all the way into the drain body when you pull up on the lift rod, adjust the pivot rod.

■ If a stopper does not hold water, remove it and clean the rubber seal. If there is an O-ring, replace it, or replace the stopper.

■ If water leaks from the pivot rod, tighten the nut. If that doesn't work, remove the pivot rod and replace the gaskets.

PRESTART CHECKLIST

☐ **TIME**
An hour or so for most repairs

☐ **TOOLS**
Groove-joint pliers, screwdriver, long-nose pliers

☐ **SKILLS**
No special skills needed

☐ **PREP**
Make the work area comfortable. Place a bucket under the assembly to catch water.

☐ **MATERIALS**
Plumber's putty, replacement 1¼-inch rubber or plastic washers, perhaps new gaskets, perhaps a new drain assembly

Adjusting the stopper

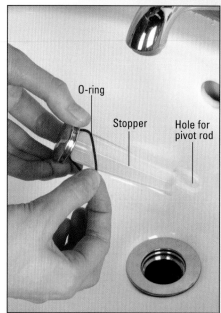

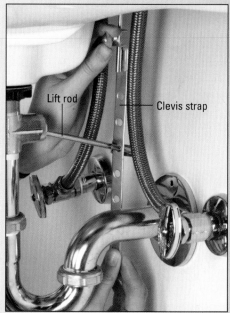

1 Some stoppers can be removed simply by pulling up. With others you twist a quarter-turn or so, then lift up. A third type has a hole through which the pivot rod passes (shown above); remove the pivot rod first. Check the O-ring for damage; remove and replace it if necessary.

2 To adjust a stopper up or down, loosen the lift rod nut with your fingers or with a pair of long-nose pliers if it is corroded. Slide the clevis strap up or down as needed, tighten the nut, and test.

BATHROOM DRAIN ASSEMBLY

A pop-up assembly only looks complicated. A pivot rod, connected to the lift rod with a clevis strap, raises and lowers the stopper.

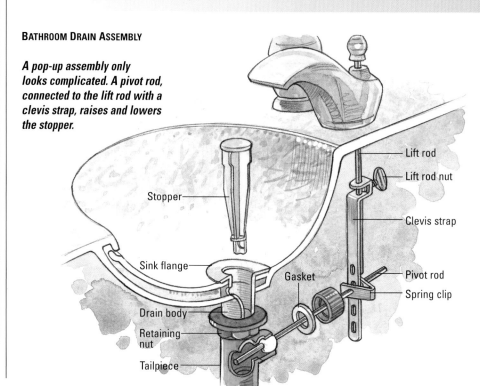

Replacing a drain body

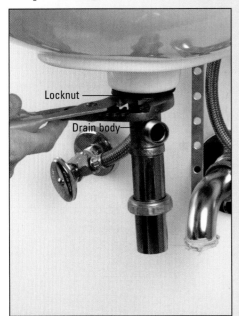

1 Disconnect the trap *(page 24)*. Slide the clevis strap off the pivot rod, loosen the retaining nut, and remove the pivot rod. Insert a screwdriver into the drain opening in the sink to keep it from turning, and loosen the locknut with pliers.

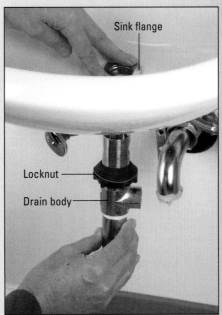

2 Unscrew the locknut. Push down on the sink flange with one hand while you unscrew the drain body with the other.

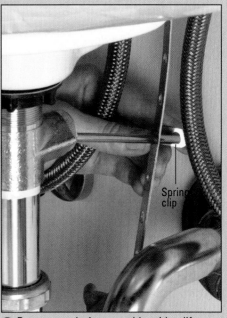

3 Buy a new drain assembly with a lift rod that fits through your faucet, or buy a new faucet and drain body. Slip the sink flange through the hole in the sink and screw on the drain body. Tighten the locknut, install the pivot rod, attach it to the clevis strap with the spring clip, and adjust.

STANLEY PRO TIP

Easy fix for a leaking drain body

You may need to tighten the retaining nut on a pivot rod from time to time, either to seal a leak or to keep a stopper from falling down when it's supposed to stay up.

REFRESHER COURSE
Dismantling a trap

Use a pair of groove-joint pliers to loosen the slip nuts on the curved trap piece. Slide the nuts and rubber washer out of the way and pull the pieces apart. Unless the rubber washers are in pristine condition, replace them. If the trap is damaged, replace it.

WHAT IF...
There is no rubber gasket?

A bathroom sink flange may come with a rubber gasket that seals it to the sink. If not, apply a rope of plumber's putty to the underside of the flange before installing it. Excess putty will squeeze out as you tighten the locknut.

KITCHEN BASKET STRAINER

If water leaks from under the sink, the basket strainer may not be tightly sealed. To test, close the stopper, fill the sink with water, and inspect from underneath with a flashlight and a dry rag.

If the strainer leaks, try tightening the locknut using groove-joint pliers or a spud wrench (*page 35*). If that doesn't solve the problem, remove the strainer, following the steps on these pages. Either clean the drain hole and reinstall the strainer or install a new strainer.

A cheap strainer made of thin metal or plastic may soon fail to seal water. Spend a little more for a better quality strainer that will last longer.

Installation is the same no matter what the sink material—stainless steel, cast iron, or acrylic.

PRESTART CHECKLIST

☐ **TIME**
About 2 hours to remove a basket strainer and install a new one

☐ **TOOLS**
Groove-joint pliers, spud wrench, plastic putty knife, hammer

☐ **SKILLS**
Dismantling and reinstalling a trap (*pages 24–25*)

☐ **PREP**
Make the work site under the sink comfortable. Position a bucket to catch water.

☐ **MATERIALS**
New basket strainer, plumber's putty, replacement 1½-inch rubber or plastic washers

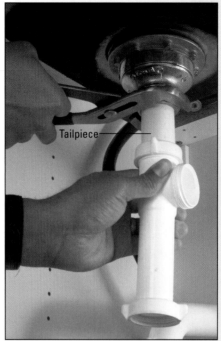

Tailpiece

1 Unscrew the slip nuts at the bottom and top of the tailpiece. Gently pull the tailpiece down from the strainer and remove it. Unless the washers are in very good condition, buy replacement washers. If any part of the trap is damaged, replace it as well.

Locknut

2 Loosen the locknut with groove-joint pliers or a spud wrench (*page 35*). Remove the nut, and pull out the strainer. Scrape the old putty away from around the sink hole, and clean with a rag.

KITCHEN SINK STRAINERS

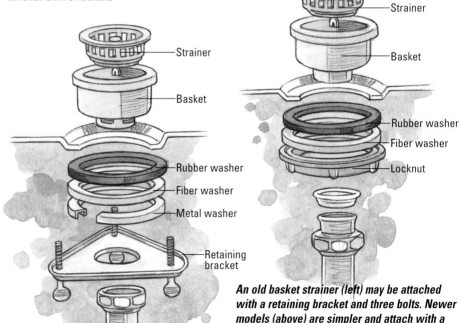

Strainer

Basket

Rubber washer

Fiber washer

Metal washer

Retaining bracket

Strainer

Basket

Rubber washer

Fiber washer

Locknut

An old basket strainer (left) may be attached with a retaining bracket and three bolts. Newer models (above) are simpler and attach with a locknut.

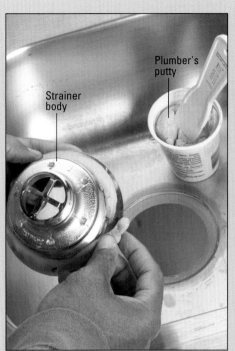

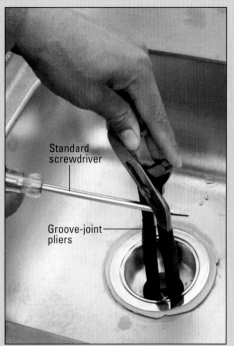

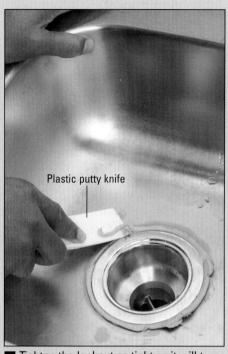

3 Make a rope of plumber's putty (do not use putty that has started to dry), and place it around the sink hole or under the lip of the strainer body. Press the strainer body into the hole and center it.

4 Have a helper hold the strainer in place while you slip on the rubber washer, the cardboard washer, and the locknut. To keep the strainer from spinning while you tighten the locknut, insert the handles of a pair of pliers into the holes and brace them with a screwdriver.

5 Tighten the locknut as tight as it will turn. Scrape away the squeezed-out putty with a plastic putty knife to avoid scratching the sink. Reattach the tailpiece. To test for leaks, close the stopper, fill the sink, then pull out the stopper.

WHAT IF...
There is a leak from the garbage disposer?

A garbage disposer comes with its own strainer. If water leaks from above the disposer (that is, at the point where the disposer attaches to the sink), tighten the mounting ring screws. If that doesn't solve the problem, remove the disposer, disconnect the flange, clean the hole around the sink, and install a new rope of putty.

If water leaks from the connection where the drain meets the disposer, tighten the two screws. You may need to replace the rubber gasket inside. If water seeps from the disposer itself, replace the disposer.

Got a disposer?
For instructions on installing a new trap and disposer for a kitchen sink, see *pages 78–79*.

Get a grip with a spud wrench

Tightening and loosening a basket strainer's locknut is difficult because the nut is large and hard to reach. A pair of groove-joint pliers does the trick but may be cumbersome. A spud wrench (below) or a special basket-strainer wrench makes the job easier.

If the nut is very tight, place the tip of a screwdriver against one of its lugs and tap with a hammer until it loosens.

FAUCETS

A leaky faucet is the most common household plumbing problem. A house call by a professional plumber will cost plenty, so it makes sense to fix it yourself. This chapter explains how to stop sink and bathtub faucets from dripping from the spout or oozing water from the base of the handle.

Shut off the water

The first step is to stop the flow of water to the faucet (see *pages 6–7*). If there is a pair of stop valves under a sink, turn them off. If there are no stop valves, look for intermediate shutoff valves elsewhere in the house. Failing that, you may have to shut off water to the entire house.

Some bathtub faucets have integrated shutoffs. Look for an access panel behind the tub; shutoff valves may be inside. If not, you'll need to shut off intermediate valves or water to the whole house.

After shutting off the water, open the faucet and wait for the water to stop running. If the faucet is on the first floor of a multistory house, you may have to wait a minute or so for the water to drain.

If the house has old galvanized pipes, shutting the water off and turning it back on will probably dislodge debris inside the pipes, clogging aerators in faucets and showerheads throughout the house; see *pages 20–21* for how to clean them.

Finding the right parts

You may spend more time finding the correct parts than working on the faucet. To prevent multiple shopping trips, remove the worn parts—perhaps even the whole faucet—and take them with you to the store.

The faucets shown in this chapter are the most common types. Chances are good that yours will look and work much like one of them. However, hundreds of faucet types have been made, so you could have an unusual model with parts that are hard to find.

A helpful and competent salesperson can save you plenty of time. Some home centers have knowledgeable people. The staff at a local hardware store may have more expertise. Plumbing supply stores, which cater to professionals, can be impatient with do-it-yourselfers, but they have a wide selection of parts as well as knowledgeable personnel.

If your faucet has a brand name inscribed on its body, look for a repair kit to match. Otherwise, dismantle the faucet to find out its type. Read the relevant repair instructions *(pages 38–55)* to determine which parts need replacement.

In some cases, only inexpensive O-rings and washers are needed. Other times, the basic guts—a cartridge, stem, or ball, for instance—need to be replaced. Usually replacing the inner workings results in a faucet that works as smoothly and is as durable as a new faucet.

Fix or replace?

If parts are hard to find or expensive, or if the faucet is unattractive, you may be better off replacing the whole faucet rather than repairing it; *pages 60–65* show how. Depending on the type and age of the faucet, replacing may take less time.

Other leaks

If water leaks below the sink, the problem may be a leaky stop valve or supply tube *(pages 108–109)*. If the leak is at the point where the supply tube enters the faucet, try tightening the nut. If that doesn't solve the problem, replace the supply tube.

If you can find the parts, most faucet repairs are easy. Otherwise consider installing a new unit.

CHAPTER PREVIEW

Sink faucet repairs
page 38

Tub and shower faucet repairs
page 50

Diverters
page 56

Tub spouts
page 57

At a hardware store or home center, you will find a rack of repair kits that covers the most common faucet types. If you don't find the right parts, they can probably be ordered. Failing that, consider replacing the entire faucet set.

Repair kit

Replacement O-ring

Replacement washer

Worn washer

Installing a flex-line shower unit
page 58

Kitchen sprayers
page 59

Installing a kitchen faucet
page 60

Installing a bathroom faucet
page 64

Before installing a new rubber part, check that it is an exact duplicate of the old part. Worn washers (above) or O-rings are the most common cause of run-on faucets. They come in a wide variety of shapes and sizes, even within the same brand, so always bring the worn part along when you're shopping for a replacement.

STEM (COMPRESSION) FAUCETS

Most older two-handle faucets have stems that move up and down when a handle is turned. A rubber washer at the bottom of the stem presses against a seat in the faucet body to seal out water. If the washer or the seat becomes worn, water seeps through and drips out of the spout. If water seeps below the handle or the base of the faucet, an O-ring or the packing probably needs to be replaced.

Getting the parts

All-purpose repair kits for stem faucets contain washers and O-rings of various sizes. To make sure you have a perfect match, take the stem along when buying the repair kit. An older type of faucet may need a packing washer or string packing. If the stem itself is worn, replacing the rubber parts will not solve the problem. You can replace the stem, but it may be hard to find; replacing the faucet is usually the best option.

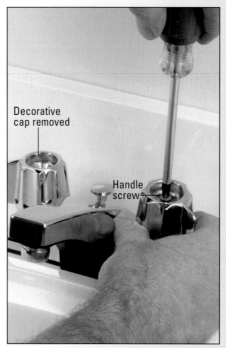

Decorative cap removed

Handle screw

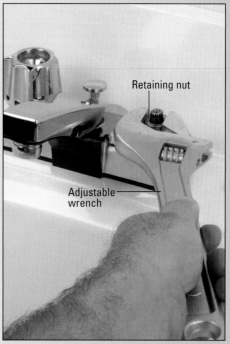

Retaining nut

Adjustable wrench

1 **Shut off the water** and open both handles until water stops running. Pry off the decorative cap (if any), remove the handle screw, and gently pry off the handle. If the handle is stuck, try tapping and prying on one side, then the other, or use a handle puller *(page 39)*.

2 Use an adjustable wrench to loosen and remove the retaining or packing nut. A sleeve may also cover the stem. Grab the stem with a pair of pliers and pull it out.

PRESTART CHECKLIST

☐ **TIME**
Less than an hour for most repairs

☐ **TOOLS**
Screwdrivers, adjustable wrench, groove-joint pliers, possibly a handle puller, seat wrench, or seat grinder

☐ **SKILLS**
Shutting off water, dismantling a faucet, installing small parts

☐ **PREP**
Shut off the water, close the sink stopper, and place a rag in the sink to catch any parts.

☐ **MATERIALS**
Washer, O-rings, packing, silicone grease

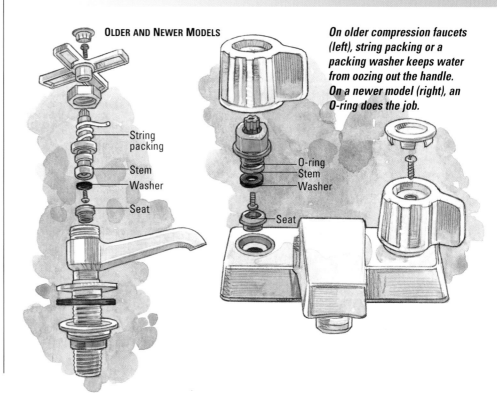

OLDER AND NEWER MODELS

String packing

Stem

Washer

Seat

O-ring
Stem
Washer

Seat

On older compression faucets (left), string packing or a packing washer keeps water from oozing out the handle. On a newer model (right), an O-ring does the job.

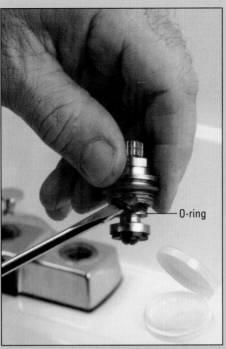

Washer

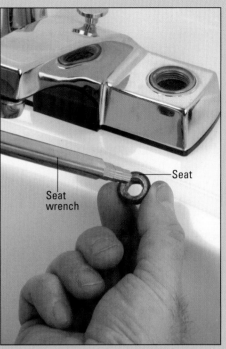

O-ring

Seat

Seat wrench

3 If water drips out the spout when the handle is turned off, you probably need to replace a worn washer. Remove the screw and install an exact replacement. If this doesn't solve the problem, or if washers wear out quickly, replace the seat (Step 5).

4 If water seeps out below the handle, replace a worn O-ring or any other rubber part on the stem. Gently pry out the O-ring with a knife or small screwdriver. Rub silicone grease on the replacement O-ring and reinstall it.

5 If the seat is pitted or scratched, remove it using a seat wrench *(page 9)*. Install an exact replacement. If you can't find a new seat, you may be able to grind a worn seat.

WHAT IF...
The handle is stuck?

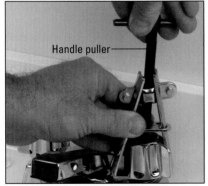

Handle puller

Handles on older two-handle faucets may be stuck tight. If tapping and prying with moderate pressure does not remove a handle, avoid the temptation to pry hard—you may crack the handle or the faucet body. A handle puller grasps the handle from underneath at two sides and slowly draws the handle off the stem.

STANLEY PRO TIP

Use packing on old stems

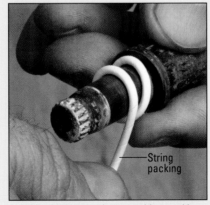

String packing

An older faucet may have a rubber packing washer or string packing under a packing nut. If water leaks out the handle, clean out the old packing and install a new packing washer, or wrap string packing around the stem and cram it up into the packing nut.

GRIND A WORN SEAT
Using a seat grinder

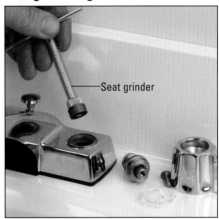

Seat grinder

If you cannot obtain a new seat, try using a seat grinder to smooth the existing seat. Keep the tool stable while you grind; if it wobbles, you may make matters worse. The seat should be smooth and even when you're done.

REVERSE-COMPRESSION FAUCETS

This two-handle faucet looks like a stem faucet but operates by opening and closing in the opposite direction. The seat is attached to the bottom of the stem body. The washer attaches to the bottom of the spindle and faces upward. When the faucet is opened, the spindle moves downward, creating a gap between the seat and the washer.

Getting the parts

Chicago (shown in Steps 1–5) and Crane (shown on *page 41*) are among the companies that make this type of faucet. Be sure to get parts made specifically for your model. Washers may be different in shape, so a standard stem washer may appear to fit, but it will not properly seal. Repair kits typically have O-rings, seats, and washers, so you can replace all the non-metal parts. Often, however, all you need is the washer.

PRESTART CHECKLIST

☐ **TIME**
Less than an hour for most repairs

☐ **TOOLS**
Screwdrivers, adjustable wrench, groove-joint pliers, possibly a handle puller

☐ **SKILLS**
Shutting off water, dismantling a faucet, installing small parts

☐ **PREP**
Shut off the water, close the sink stopper, and place a rag in the sink to catch any parts.

☐ **MATERIALS**
Washer, seat, and O-rings for your faucet

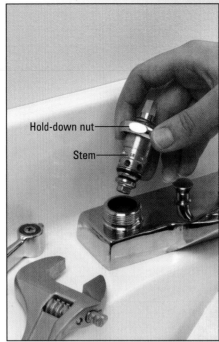

1 **Shut off the water** and open both handles until water stops flowing. Remove the handle *(pages 38–39)*. Use an adjustable wrench to loosen the hold-down nut. Unscrew and remove the stem.

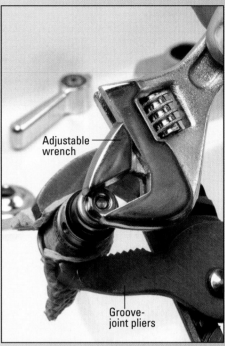

2 Grasp the stem with groove-joint pliers, using a cloth in the jaws to prevent scratches. Use an adjustable wrench to loosen and remove the nut at the bottom; the seat will not slide out. On models with no bottom nut, twist the seat to remove it.

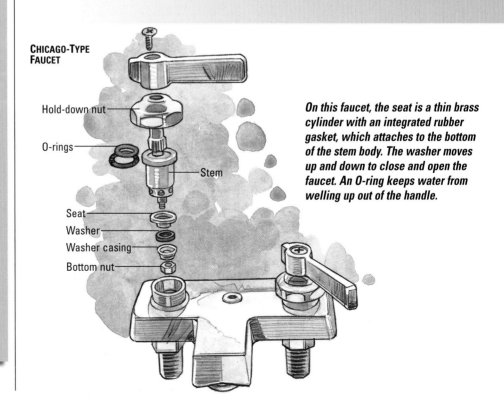

CHICAGO-TYPE FAUCET

Hold-down nut
O-rings
Stem
Seat
Washer
Washer casing
Bottom nut

On this faucet, the seat is a thin brass cylinder with an integrated rubber gasket, which attaches to the bottom of the stem body. The washer moves up and down to close and open the faucet. An O-ring keeps water from welling up out of the handle.

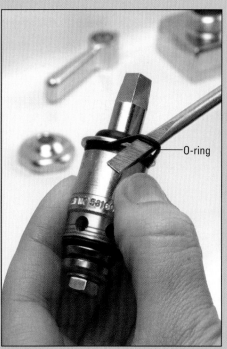

3 If the seat looks worn, replace it. Depending on the the type of faucet, either slip or twist it into position.

4 Replace the washer. Be sure to install one that is made for your faucet.

5 If water wells up below the handle while water is running, or if an O-ring looks worn, replace it with an exact duplicate.

WHAT IF...
You have a Crane reverse-compression faucet?

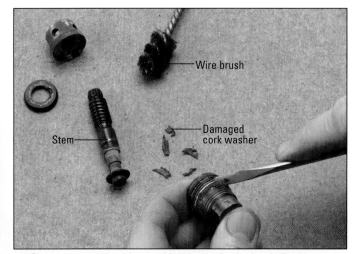

1 The other prominent maker of reverse-compression faucets is Crane. Remove a Crane stem as you would on a Chicago model. Twist the top portion to unscrew it from the bottom portion.

2 Clean away debris with a toothbrush or soft wire brush. Remove rubber and cork parts. Install exact replacements (the replacement for a cork ring may be made of rubber). Rub silicone grease on the large threads before reassembling.

Two-Handle Cartridge (Disk) and Diaphragm Faucets

Many newer two-handle faucets, including models made by Price-Pfister, Sterling, Kohler, and Moen, use either individual cartridges or diaphragm stems. Both types are long-lived and easy to repair.

An individual cartridge is similar to a single-handle cartridge *(page 48)*. It contains a plastic or rubber valve that opens and closes to permit or stop the flow of water.

Fixing a leaky faucet may require replacing the cartridge or replacing O-rings and seals, depending on the manufacturer and model.

Prestart Checklist

☐ **Time**
Less than an hour for most repairs

☐ **Tools**
Screwdrivers, adjustable wrench, groove-joint pliers, possibly a socket wrench, and a handle puller

☐ **Skills**
Shutting off water, dismantling a faucet, installing small parts

☐ **Prep**
Shut off the water, close the sink stopper, and place a rag in the sink to catch any parts.

☐ **Materials**
Repair kit for your faucet model, silicone grease

1 **Shut off the water.** Turn the handles on to drain out any water. The handle may be held with a top screw *(page 38)*, or it may twist off. Wrap the handle with a cloth before twisting it with groove-joint pliers.

2 Pull the cartridge up and out. With some types, it is important to note which direction the cartridge is facing so you can reinstall it facing the same direction. You may need to use a socket wrench, pliers, or even a special pulling tool made for certain brands of stems *(page 49)*.

Price-Pfister, Sterling/Rockwell Types

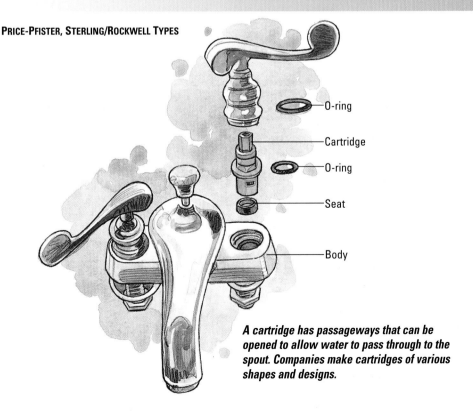

A cartridge has passageways that can be opened to allow water to pass through to the spout. Companies make cartridges of various shapes and designs.

Seat

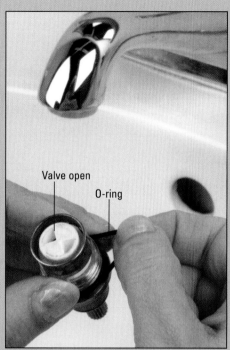

Valve open

O-ring

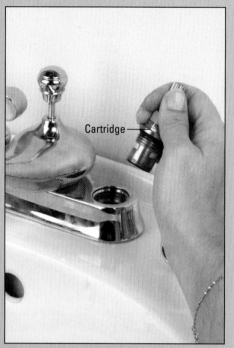

Cartridge

3 If the cartridge is metal, replacing the rubber parts usually fixes the problem. Pry off the rubber seat at the bottom.

4 Twist the cartridge spindle so the valve opens. Wash out any debris. If the internal parts are worn, replace the cartridge. Replace the rubber seat and any O-rings. Rub the parts with silicone grease.

5 Install the cartridge and the handle and test. If you cannot turn the water on or off, remove and reorient the cartridge.

Diaphragm faucet

A diaphragm faucet has two stems similar to those in a standard stem faucet (pages 38–39). However, the stem has a neoprene cap, called a diaphragm, at the bottom instead of a washer. Usually you can simply pry off the diaphragm and slip on a new one. If that does not fix a leak, replace the stem or the faucet.

Stem

Diaphragm

Seat

TWO-HANDLE DISK FAUCET

A two-handle disk faucet uses disk assemblies similar to one in a single-handle disk faucet, and also has springs similar to those in a ball faucet.

Handle

Locknut

Mounting screw

Disk assembly installed

Disk assembly

Seat

Spring

SINGLE-HANDLE DISK (CERAMIC DISK) FAUCETS

A single-handle disk faucet made by American Standard, Peerless, and Reliant, among others, is made with a pair of ceramic or plastic disks encased in a cylinder. The upper disk rotates when you turn the handle. Water flows when the inlets of the upper and lower disks line up.

Getting the parts

If water wells up around the handle or drips out of the spout, replace the seals with exact duplicates. If that does not solve the problem, replace the entire cylinder—you cannot open it up to replace disks. If water flow is slow or erratic, particles of rust and minerals may be clogging the inlets. Cleaning them solves the problem.

PRESTART CHECKLIST

☐ **TIME**
Less than an hour for most repairs

☐ **TOOLS**
Screwdriver, adjustable wrench, groove-joint pliers, hex wrench, cleaning brush

☐ **SKILLS**
Shutting off water, dismantling a faucet, installing small parts

☐ **PREP**
Shut off the water, close the sink stopper, and place a rag in the sink to catch any parts.

☐ **MATERIALS**
Repair kit with seals and O-rings, silicone grease

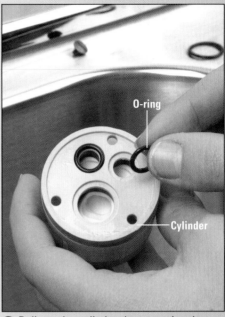

1 **Shut off the water.** Turn the faucet on until the water stops running. To remove the handle, you'll probably need to unscrew a setscrew using a hex wrench or small screwdriver. Lift off the handle and remove the dome housing.

2 Pull out the cylinder that contains the disks and take it to a home center or hardware store to find replacement parts. The O-rings can be pried out of the cylinder using your fingers.

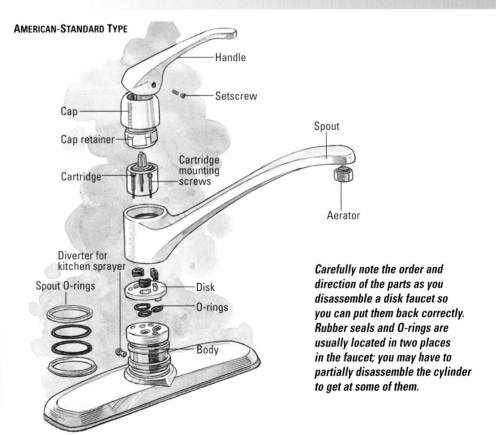

AMERICAN-STANDARD TYPE

Carefully note the order and direction of the parts as you disassemble a disk faucet so you can put them back correctly. Rubber seals and O-rings are usually located in two places in the faucet; you may have to partially disassemble the cylinder to get at some of them.

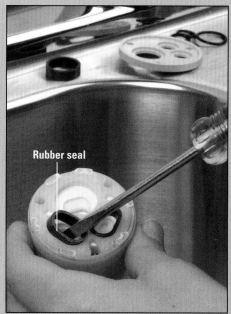

Rubber seal

3 On some models, removing the bottom plate reveals the rubber seals. Remove them with a small screwdriver, taking care not to nick the plastic housing. If the cylinder is cracked or scored, replace it. Otherwise buy a kit with the rubber seals and O-rings.

4 Before replacing the rubber parts, gently clean away scum and debris from the seats, using a toothbrush or a nonmetallic abrasive pad. Rub a little silicone grease on the rubber parts.

5 Reassemble the cylinder. Install the cylinder so it faces the same direction as it did before.

Disk faucet with gaskets

Instead of individual O-rings or rubber seals, some disk faucets use a rubber or nylon gasket. This way only one part is needed rather than two or three separate parts. To repair, simply replace the worn gasket.

WHAT IF...
The faucet leaks at the base?

Some single-handle disk faucets have large rubber rings at the base of the spout. These may wear out. Remove the worn rings with a standard screwdriver or knife. Take the old ring with you to find an exact replacement.

Clean away any debris, coat the replacement parts with silicone grease, and reinstall.

To repair the diverter and the kitchen sprayer, see *page 59*.

If water drips below the faucet and you find wet spots in the cabinet floor, feel with your hand and check with a flashlight to find the highest wet spot. You may need to tighten a supply tube where it hooks to the faucet.

BALL FAUCETS

On the outside, this single-handle faucet (made by Delta and others) looks a lot like a disk faucet, but it has a narrower cylinder under the handle. Inside is a metal or plastic ball with grooves and holes. When the handle turns, the grooves or holes line up with rubber-sealed inlets in the faucet body to allow water to flow.

This type of faucet can become clogged by small particles. If water flow is slow or erratic, disassemble and clean the inlets.

Getting the parts

If water seeps out below the handle or drips out the spout, tighten the cap or the cap-adjusting ring. If that does not solve the problem, buy a rebuild kit for your model.

If water seeps out the base of the faucet, replace the O-rings. If water drips from the spout, replace the seats and springs. Less commonly, a ball is damaged and needs to be replaced.

PRESTART CHECKLIST

☐ **TIME**
Less than an hour for most repairs

☐ **TOOLS**
Screwdriver, adjustable wrench, groove-joint pliers, hex wrench

☐ **SKILLS**
Shutting off water, dismantling a faucet, installing small parts

☐ **PREP**
Shut off the water, close the sink stopper, and place a rag in the sink to catch any parts.

☐ **MATERIALS**
Repair kit (including O-rings, seats, springs, and other plastic parts), perhaps a new ball

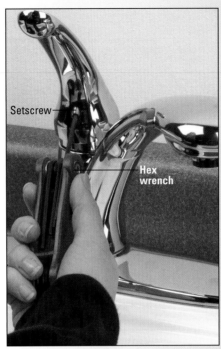

1 **Shut off the water** and turn the faucet on until water stops running. Loosen the handle setscrew with a hex wrench, sometimes included in a repair kit. Lift off the handle and unscrew the cap.

2 Remove the plastic cam and lift out the ball. If the ball is worn, replace it along with the seats and springs.

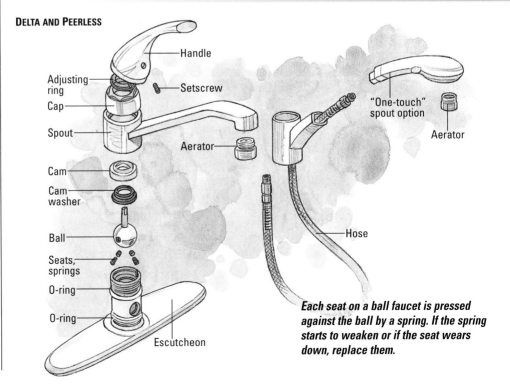

DELTA AND PEERLESS

Each seat on a ball faucet is pressed against the ball by a spring. If the spring starts to weaken or if the seat wears down, replace them.

Seat

3 Carefully insert the tip of a screwdriver into a seat and pull it out. This may take a couple of tries for each seat.

Spring

4 Use the same technique to remove the springs. Clean or flush out debris in the faucet body. Purchase springs and seats for your faucet model.

5 Replace the springs and seats, and press them into place with your finger. Insert the ball so it sits snugly. Add the washer and screw on the adjusting ring. You may need a special wrench to tighten the ring. If the faucet still leaks, tighten the ring further.

WHAT IF...
You find debris?

If small particles partially clog the inlets, first wipe away as much as you can. Slowly turn the water back on to flush out more particles. If you have old galvanized pipes, you may need to do this regularly.

O-rings at the base

To cure a leak at the base of the faucet below the handle, pull or twist off the spout. Pry or cut off the old O-rings, coat the faucet body lightly with silicone grease, and slip on the new O-rings. When you reattach the spout, make sure it slides all the way down.

STANLEY PRO TIP

Metal or plastic ball?

An inexpensive plastic ball is easily scratched, so it may wear out in less than a year, especially if your water contains debris. A metal ball is worth the extra cost because it lasts longer.

CARTRIDGE FAUCETS

Several manufacturers, including Moen, Price-Pfister, Delta, Peerless, and Kohler, make single-handle cartridge faucets. Each model has a cartridge of a slightly different design. A cartridge may have a cylinder with grooves, or it may be tapered so water can pass through when it is turned.

Getting the parts

If water leaks out the spout, you'll have to replace or repair the cartridge. If a leaky faucet's cartridge is plastic, replace it; if it is metal, you may need to replace only the O-rings. If water wells up below the handle, replace the O-rings around the faucet body. Many repair kits contain both the cartridge and the O-rings.

PRESTART CHECKLIST

☐ **TIME**
Less than an hour for most repairs

☐ **TOOLS**
Screwdrivers, adjustable wrench, groove-joint pliers, hex wrench

☐ **SKILLS**
Shutting off water, dismantling a faucet, installing small parts

☐ **PREP**
Shut off the water, close the sink stopper, and place a rag in the sink to catch any parts.

☐ **MATERIALS**
Replacement cartridge or repair kit for your model, silicone grease

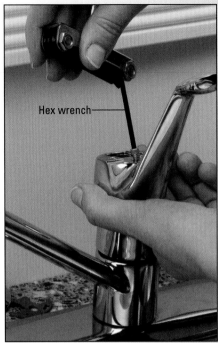

Hex wrench

1 **Shut off the water.** Turn on the faucet until the water stops running. To remove the handle, pry off the decorative cap and remove the screw, using a hex wrench or screwdriver as needed. Lift off the handle.

Handle attachment mechanism

2 Unscrew the cap or retaining ring. If you find a handle-attachment mechanism like the one shown, note how it is attached so you can replace it correctly.

DELTA AND PEERLESS TYPES

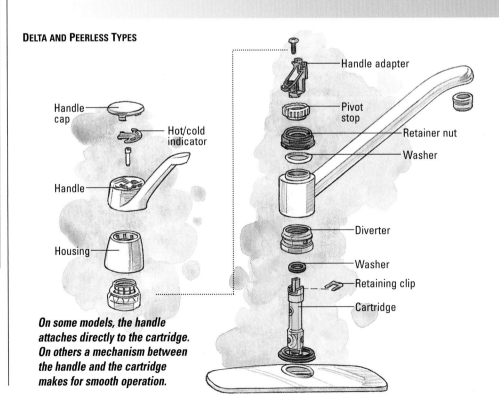

Handle cap

Hot/cold indicator

Handle

Housing

Handle adapter

Pivot stop

Retainer nut

Washer

Diverter

Washer

Retaining clip

Cartridge

On some models, the handle attaches directly to the cartridge. On others a mechanism between the handle and the cartridge makes for smooth operation.

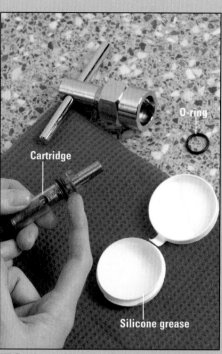

3 Many cartridges can be removed simply by pulling up with pliers. If it is stuck, you may need to buy a stem puller designed for your faucet.

4 Remove the spout. Pry off any damaged O-rings and replace them with duplicates. Apply a thin coat of silicone grease and replace the spout.

5 Replace either the O-rings on the cartridge or the entire cartridge. If the cartridge is not already greasy, apply a thin coat of grease and push it into position.

STANLEY PRO TIP

Special pullers

Some faucets have cartridges that can be removed only with a manufacturer-specific pulling tool. Trying to remove the cartridge without the proper tool can damage the cartridge and faucet.

Other cartridges

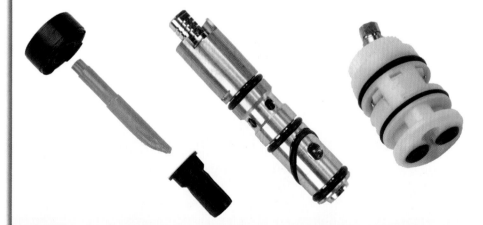

A plastic cartridge made by Kohler (left) slips into a cartridge casing; make sure it is well greased. If hot and cold are reversed after installing it, remove the cartridge and turn it

180 degrees. A brass cartridge (center) requires several O-rings of two different sizes. Another type (right) uses O-rings as well as rubber seats.

TUB AND SHOWER STEM COMPRESSION FAUCETS

Tub and shower faucets work much like sink faucets, but they are oriented horizontally rather than vertically. In addition, their parts are usually larger. A two-handle stem shower faucet has a stem with a washer that presses against a seat to seal off water, just like the faucet shown on *pages 38–39*. A three-handle unit adds a stemlike diverter to direct water up to the shower or down to the tub spout.

Getting the parts
Often leaks can be fixed simply by replacing the washers. Even if you need to replace the seats or stems, it usually makes sense to repair rather than replace an old shower faucet, because replacement requires opening up the wall. If parts are hard to find, special order them at a plumbing supply store.

PRESTART CHECKLIST

☐ **TIME**
An hour or two for most repairs

☐ **TOOLS**
Screwdrivers, adjustable wrench, groove-joint pliers, perhaps a stem socket wrench, seat wrench

☐ **SKILLS**
Shutting off water, dismantling a faucet, installing small parts

☐ **PREP**
Shut off the water, close the tub stopper, and place a rag in the tub to catch any loose parts.

☐ **MATERIALS**
Washers, O-rings, perhaps new stems

1 **Shut off the water** *(pages 6–7).* Turn both handles on until water stops flowing. Pry off the handle cap, remove the screw, and pry off the handle. You may need to use a handle puller *(page 39).* Unscrew the stem sleeve and pull off the escutcheon.

2 If the stem protrudes far enough past the wall surface, loosen it with an adjustable wrench or groove-joint pliers. If the stem is recessed, use a stem wrench.

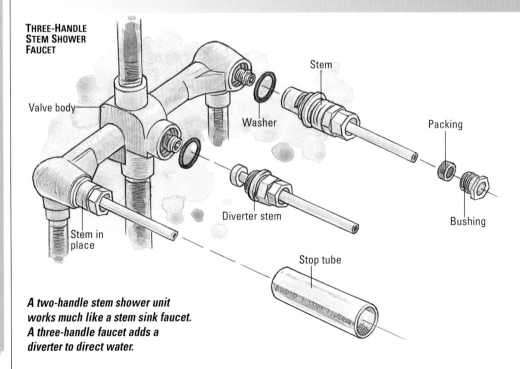

THREE-HANDLE STEM SHOWER FAUCET

A two-handle stem shower unit works much like a stem sink faucet. A three-handle faucet adds a diverter to direct water.

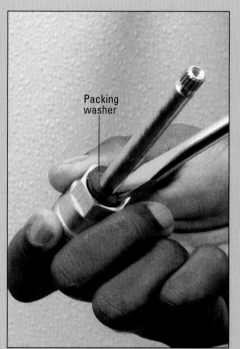

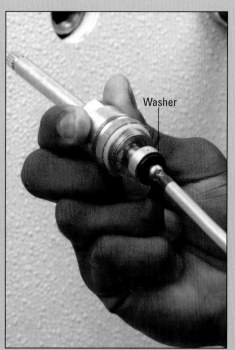

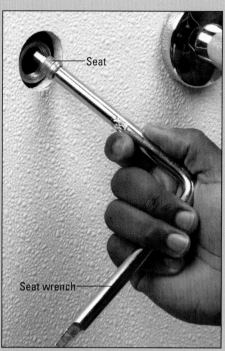

3 If water seeps out around the handle, replace a worn packing washer or stuff thread packing around the stem and into the cavity behind the packing nut *(page 39)*.

4 If water drips out the spout or the showerhead, replace a worn washer with an exact duplicate.

5 If replacing the washer does not stop the leak or if washers wear out quickly, remove the seat with a seat wrench and replace it. Or grind the seat smooth with a seat grinder *(page 39)*.

RECESSED
Using a stem wrench

If the stem nut is behind the wall, you won't be able to unscrew the stem with an adjustable wrench or pliers. Use a stem wrench, a deep socket wrench made to fit a bathtub stem.

Repairing a diverter

The diverter on a three-handle tub faucet is essentially a stem. When its washer presses against the seat, water cannot rise up to the showerhead and is diverted to the tub spout.

You repair a diverter in much the same way as you do a hot or cold stem. Replace the washer at the bottom and replace any O-rings and other removable parts.

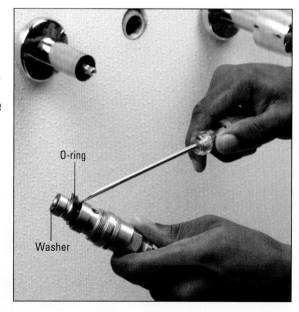

TUB AND SHOWER CARTRIDGE FAUCETS

Once you shut off the water and remove the handle and escutcheon, you can quickly determine whether your single-handle tub and shower faucet is a cartridge, ball, or disk type *(pages 54–55)*.

Getting the parts

Tub cartridge faucets work just like sink cartridge faucets *(pages 48–49)*. Usually the faucet only turns water on and off; a diverter valve on the spout directs water to the showerhead or the spout. A number of manufacturers make cartridges of varying designs, so take the cartridge with you when you shop for parts. You may need to replace the entire cartridge. Follow the steps as shown to remove.

PRESTART CHECKLIST

☐ **TIME**
An hour or two for most repairs

☐ **TOOLS**
Screwdriver, adjustable wrench, groove-joint pliers, hex wrench, cartridge puller

☐ **SKILLS**
Shutting off water, dismantling a faucet, installing small parts

☐ **PREP**
Shut off the water, close the tub stopper, and place a rag in the tub to catch any parts.

☐ **MATERIALS**
Cartridge or repair kit for your faucet model, silicone grease

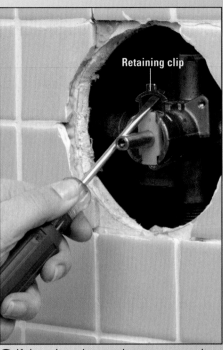

1 **Shut off the water** *(pages 6–7)* and turn the faucet on until water stops running. To remove the handle, you may need a hex wrench, which is sometimes included in a repair kit. Remove the screws holding the escutcheon and slide out the escutcheon.

2 If there is a chrome sleeve, unscrew it or pull it out. Use a small screwdriver to pry out the retaining clip that holds the cartridge in place.

MOEN, KOHLER/BRADLEY TYPE

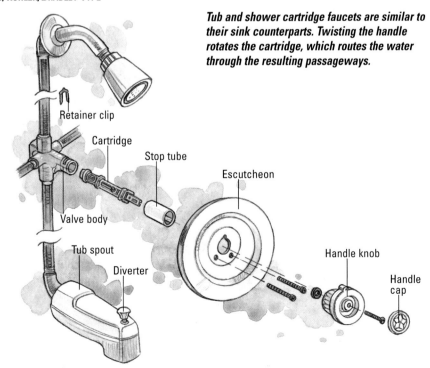

Tub and shower cartridge faucets are similar to their sink counterparts. Twisting the handle rotates the cartridge, which routes the water through the resulting passageways.

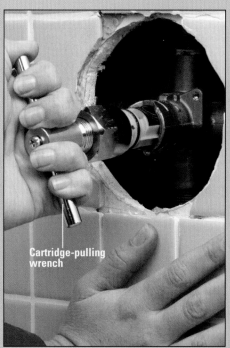

3 Some cartridges can be removed easily with pliers; others require a special cartridge-pulling wrench (usually available at hardware stores or home centers) made for a specific brand of faucet.

4 If the cartridge is in good shape, replace the O-rings and any other replaceable parts. (Often, however, it doesn't cost much more to replace the cartridge.) Rub the O-rings with a thin coat of silicone grease.

5 Insert the new or repaired cartridge into the faucet body, oriented as it was originally. Slide in the retaining clip and replace the handle and escutcheon.

WHAT IF...
You find this cartridge?

This cartridge works by virtue of its tapered shape, rather than a series of grooves. Take careful note of the cartridge's orientation when you remove it so you can put it back the same way. If hot and cold water are reversed after you reinstall the cartridge, twist it 180 degrees.

Antiscald faucets

A short burst of scalding water can be painful and even dangerous, especially for young children. That's why plumbing codes may require new tub and shower faucets to have a mechanism that prevents the passage of very hot water. Some temperature-balancing or antiscald faucets may prevent cold water from being turned off; others may have a thermostatic device that closes the hot-water valve when it senses the water is too hot.

It's hard to tell from just looking at a faucet whether it is an antiscald model. Sometimes by rocking the faucet you'll hear a click that indicates the unit has an antiscald valve. In some cases, you can replace an older standard cartridge with an antiscald cartridge.

TUB AND SHOWER BALL FAUCETS

A ball faucet has a metal or plastic ball with grooves that allow the passage of water *(page 46)*. Small springs press rubber seats against the ball to control the flow of water. Replacing the seats and springs usually will stop a leak. The ball itself may also need to be replaced.

Sometimes a leak can be fixed simply by tightening the adjusting ring with a pair of pliers or with a special tool designed for that particular model of faucet. If water flow is slow or erratic, remove the seats and springs and run water to flush out any debris.

PRESTART CHECKLIST

☐ **TIME**
An hour or two for most repairs

☐ **TOOLS**
Screwdrivers, adjustable wrench, groove-joint pliers

☐ **SKILLS**
Shutting off water, dismantling a faucet, installing small parts

☐ **PREP**
Shut off the water, close the tub stopper, and place a rag in the tub to catch any parts.

☐ **MATERIALS**
O-rings, seats, and other rubber parts, silicone grease, perhaps a new cylinder

1 **Shut off the water** *(pages 6–7)*. Turn the faucet on until it drains. Remove the handle and escutcheon. Pry off any retaining clips, unscrew the retaining ring, and pull out the cylinder.

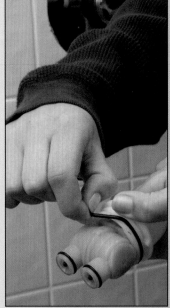

2 Take the cylinder with you to buy replacement parts. Most O-rings can be removed easily with your fingers. Replace all rubber parts. With a rag under the faucet body, slowly turn on the shutoff to flush out debris.

3 Rub silicone grease over the rubber parts. Reinsert the cylinder, reattach the retaining clip (if there is one), and screw on the adjusting ring. If the faucet leaks, tighten the ring.

Adjusting ring

DELTA/PEERLESS TYPE

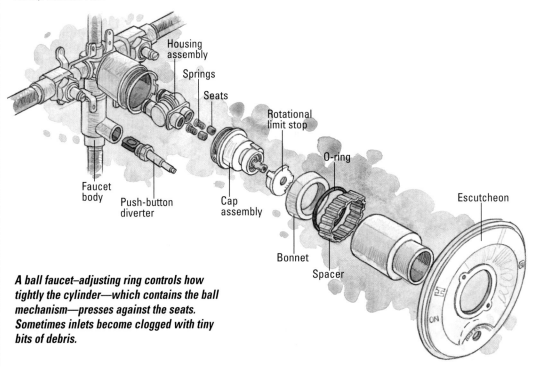

Housing assembly
Springs
Seats
Rotational limit stop
O-ring
Escutcheon
Faucet body
Push-button diverter
Cap assembly
Bonnet
Spacer

A ball faucet–adjusting ring controls how tightly the cylinder—which contains the ball mechanism—presses against the seats. Sometimes inlets become clogged with tiny bits of debris.

TUB AND SHOWER DISK FAUCET

This faucet works exactly like a sink cartridge faucet (pages 48–49). Repairs are done much the same.

If water drips out the spout or seeps out around the handle, buy a kit and replace all the rubber parts. Inspect the cylinder that contains the disks and replace it if you see signs of wear. If your model has plastic rather than ceramic disks, replace the entire unit.

Depending on the model, you may need to partially disassemble the cylinder to access all the rubber parts.

PRESTART CHECKLIST

☐ **TIME**
An hour or two for most repairs

☐ **TOOLS**
Screwdrivers, adjustable wrench, groove-joint pliers, cleaning brush

☐ **SKILLS**
Shutting off water, dismantling a faucet, installing small parts

☐ **PREP**
Shut off the water, close the tub stopper, and place a rag in the tub to catch any parts.

☐ **MATERIALS**
Repair kit for your model of faucet, silicone grease

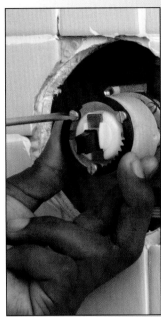

1 **Shut off the water** and turn the faucet on until water stops running. Remove the handle and the escutcheon. Unscrew three screws to remove the cylinder.

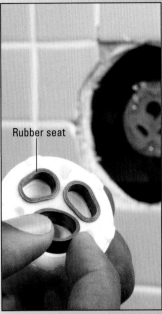

2 Remove rubber seats with your fingers. Clean the openings with a toothbrush or an abrasive pad. Replace the rubber seats with duplicates. Rub a bit of silicone grease over the seats.

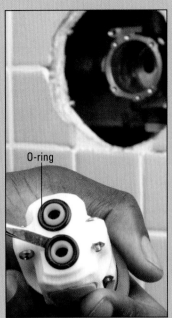

3 Do the same for all other rubber parts. If you need to pry out an O-ring, you may need to use a small screwdriver. Work carefully to prevent nicking the plastic housing.

AMERICAN STANDARD, RELIANT TYPE

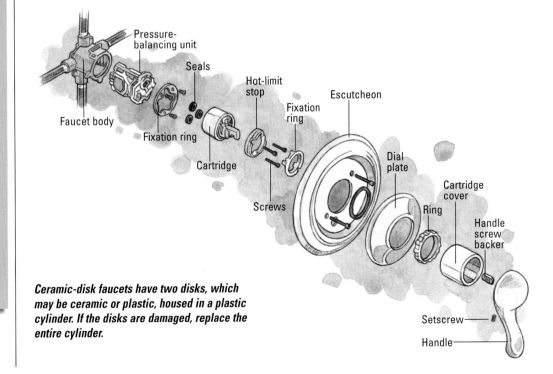

Ceramic-disk faucets have two disks, which may be ceramic or plastic, housed in a plastic cylinder. If the disks are damaged, replace the entire cylinder.

DIVERTERS

Most single-handle shower faucets simply turn water on and off; a pull-up diverter valve on the spout determines whether water goes up or down. Some models, however, have a diverter built into the handle.

Getting the parts
You may be able to find repair parts in a kit made for a specific faucet. If not, O-rings and washers made for stem faucets may fit. In some cases, the seal is made with brass parts and no washers, in which case simple cleaning and light sanding may solve the problem.

An old diverter stem may be corroded, or its spring may weaken to the point that the stem needs to be replaced. If you cannot find an old diverter stem, the home center or plumbing supply house should be able to order it. While you are waiting for the part to arrive, wrap duct tape around the handle of the diverter to keep it from going in. This will allow you to use the shower while waiting for the replacement part.

PRESTART CHECKLIST

☐ **TIME**
Less than an hour for most repairs

☐ **TOOLS**
Screwdrivers, adjustable wrench, groove-joint pliers, toothbrush

☐ **SKILLS**
Shutting off water, dismantling a faucet, installing small parts

☐ **PREP**
Shut off the water, close the tub stopper, and place a rag in the tub to catch any loose parts.

☐ **MATERIALS**
Repair kit for your faucet model, or O-rings and washers to match

Push/pull type

1 **Shut off the water** and drain the system by turning on the faucet. Remove the handle and the escutcheon. Use groove-joint pliers or an adjustable wrench to remove the diverter unit.

2 Remove and replace any worn rubber parts. If the diverter itself is worn, you may be able to buy a replacement.

BUILT-IN DIVERTER

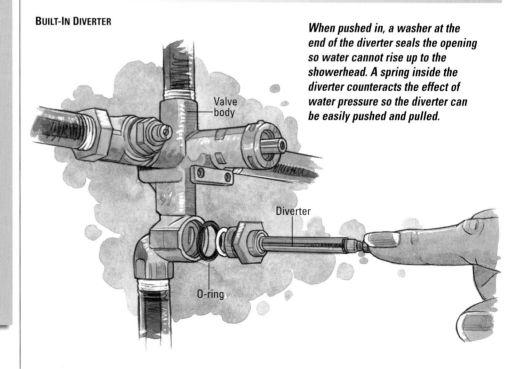

When pushed in, a washer at the end of the diverter seals the opening so water cannot rise up to the showerhead. A spring inside the diverter counteracts the effect of water pressure so the diverter can be easily pushed and pulled.

TUB SPOUTS

A tub spout may be screwed onto a threaded pipe, or it may be anchored to a nonthreaded pipe with a setscrew. Before you start to unscrew a spout, check underneath to see if there is a setscrew.

If water seeps from behind the spout, it may be attached to a threaded pipe that is not tight. Remove the pipe, wrap its threads with pipe-thread tape, and use a pipe wrench to tighten it.

If given a choice, spend a little more for a brass spout. It will last longer than a bargain-bin spout, which may be made of thin metal or even plastic that wears and stains quickly.

PRESTART CHECKLIST

☐ **TIME**
Less than an hour for most repairs

☐ **TOOLS**
Screwdrivers, hex wrench, groove-joint pliers, pipe wrench, caulk gun

☐ **SKILLS**
Unscrewing and reinstalling a spout

☐ **PREP**
There is no need to shut off the water. Place a towel in the bottom of the tub to catch any debris or caulk.

☐ **MATERIALS**
New spout, pipe-thread tape, tub-and-tile caulk

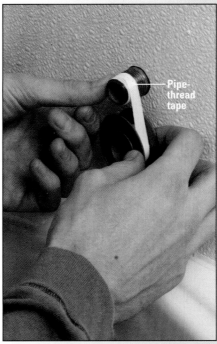

1 Use groove-joint pliers or a pipe wrench to remove an old spout that is threaded on. Clean the end of the pipe and scrape away any caulk on the wall. Wrap the pipe threads clockwise with two or three turns of pipe-thread tape.

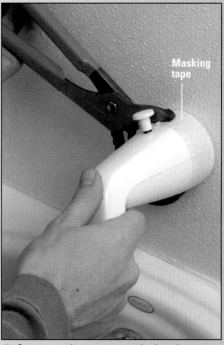

2 Screw on the new spout by hand. Wrap masking tape or a cloth around the spout, or wrap electrician's tape around the jaws of groove-joint pliers, and tighten the spout firmly. If the pipe is copper, avoid overtightening, which can strip the threads.

SETSCREW

Removing a spout held with a hex-head screw

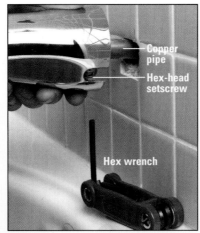

Some spouts attach with a setscrew. Loosen the screw with a hex wrench and slide off the old spout.

Spout retrofit kit

Not all spouts are created equal. Some are threaded where they meet the wall; others have threads deep in the body of the spout. You may be able to replace the pipe coming out of the wall, or purchase a retrofit kit (above) that helps make the transition.

INSTALLING A FLEX-LINE SHOWER UNIT

If your bathtub has a spout but no showerhead, installing one would be a big job. The demolition, wall repair, and tiling would take much more time than the plumbing. One solution is a flex-line shower unit. It installs quickly, and its removable showerhead is a handy feature.

If you want to install a flex-line shower, the surrounding walls should be covered with tile or another water-resistant material. If you have an old claw-foot tub that does not abut the walls, purchase a circular shower curtain.

PRESTART CHECKLIST

☐ **TIME**
About an hour for most units

☐ **TOOLS**
Drill with masonry bit, screwdriver, hammer, groove-joint pliers

☐ **SKILLS**
Drilling holes in tile, assembling parts

☐ **PREP**
There is no need to shut off the water. Place a towel in the bottom of the tub to catch any parts.

☐ **MATERIALS**
Flex-line shower unit, pipe tape, plastic anchors

Old spout

1 Remove the old spout and screw on the one that comes with the shower unit. See *page 57* for tips.

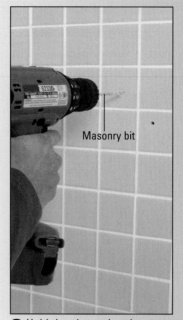

Masonry bit

2 Hold the showerhead bracket or template in place, and mark for mounting holes. Press the tip of a nail on a mark, and tap with a hammer to make a small chip as a starter hole. Drill holes with a masonry bit.

Plastic anchor

Showerhead bracket base

3 Tap plastic anchors into the holes and attach the showerhead bracket with the screws provided. Snap on its decorative body. Screw the flex line to the tub spout and slip the showerhead into the bracket.

FLEX-LINE SHOWER UNIT

This unit's spout has a diverter so water can run through the spout or up to the showerhead. Some showerheads provide a pulsating water flow.

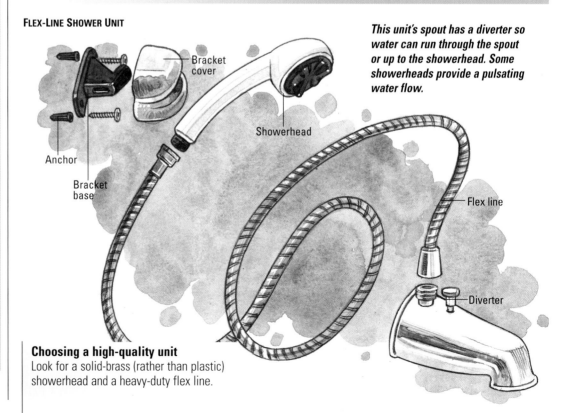

Bracket cover

Showerhead

Anchor

Bracket base

Flex line

Diverter

Choosing a high-quality unit
Look for a solid-brass (rather than plastic) showerhead and a heavy-duty flex line.

KITCHEN SPRAYERS

Kitchen sink sprayers are easy to repair. If you find that you spend a lot of time repairing the sprayer, you may want to consider purchasing a one-touch faucet *(page 63)*.

If pressure is low, check under the sink to make sure the hose is not kinked. If that's not the problem, disassemble and clean the sprayer. If that fails, turn off the water and check the diverter.

If water comes out of the sprayer even when its valve is not depressed, replace the sprayer body and valve.

PRESTART CHECKLIST

☐ **TIME**
An hour or two for most repairs

☐ **TOOLS**
Screwdriver, groove-joint pliers, long-nose pliers, knife, toothbrush

☐ **SKILLS**
Dismantling and reassembling a unit with small parts

☐ **PREP**
Shut water off only to work on the diverter valve. Lay down a small towel for organizing small parts.

☐ **MATERIALS**
Replacement parts for the sprayer and diverter, perhaps a new sprayer, silicone grease

1 Pull the sprayer out and use pliers to dismantle the spout, keeping track of all its parts. Clean them with a toothbrush. If parts are caked with minerals, soak them overnight in vinegar.

Diverter valve

2 If cleaning or replacing the sprayer does not solve the problem, **shut off the water**. Remove the spout and find the diverter valve. On this model, it is in the faucet body. Pry out the valve with a knife.

O-ring

3 Replace worn parts or the entire diverter valve. Clean away any debris, and coat the rubber parts with silicone grease. Reinstall and test. If you still have problems, consider buying a new faucet.

SPRAYER AND DIVERTER

On a disk faucet and other single-handle models (left), the diverter valve is typically placed horizontally in the faucet body. On a two-handle faucet (right), the valve is likely situated vertically in the center of the spout.

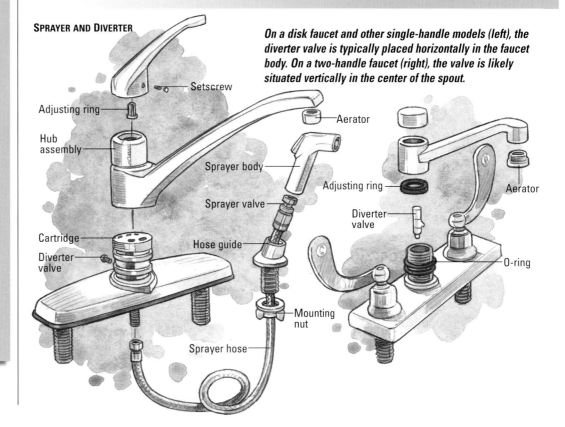

Setscrew

Adjusting ring

Hub assembly

Aerator

Sprayer body

Sprayer valve

Cartridge

Hose guide

Adjusting ring

Aerator

Diverter valve

Diverter valve

O-ring

Mounting nut

Sprayer hose

INSTALLING A KITCHEN FAUCET

The three holes in a kitchen sink accommodate most new kitchen faucets. There may be a fourth hole for a sprayer. If your faucet does not have a sprayer, consider installing a hot-water dispenser or a drinking-water faucet hooked up to a filter *(pages 80–82)*.

Installing a faucet would be easy if you didn't have to work in cramped conditions. If you are also replacing the sink, install the faucet before installing the sink *(page 68–71)*. Otherwise do what you can to make the work site comfortable *(page 19)*.

Whether you reuse the old supply tubes or buy new ones, make sure they are long enough to reach the stop valves and that they have fittings of the correct size (⅜ inch or ½ inch) for the stop valves. If there are no stop valves under the sink, now is a good time to install them *(pages 110–111)*.

Choosing a faucet

Most people find single-handle faucets easier to use. Make sure the spout is the right length for your sink. A heavy, solid-brass unit will outlast a less expensive unit. The faucet should come with a warranty that includes the sprayer.

PRESTART CHECKLIST

☐ **TIME**
About 2 hours to install most faucets

☐ **TOOLS**
Screwdriver, adjustable wrench, putty knife, groove-joint pliers, basin wrench

☐ **SKILLS**
Shutting off water, working under a sink, attaching plumbing parts

☐ **PREP**
Shut off the water to the old faucet. If the drain trap is in the way, you may have to remove it.

☐ **MATERIALS**
New faucet, plumber's putty, pipe-thread tape, masking tape

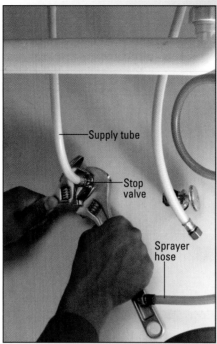

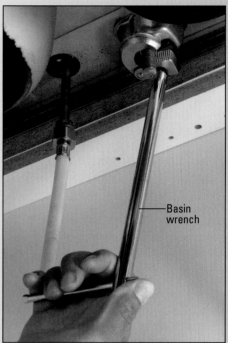

1 **Shut off the water,** and open the faucet until the water stops running. From underneath, use a wrench or pliers to hold the stop valve still while you loosen the supply tube nut with another wrench or pliers. Disconnect the sprayer hose from the faucet, or simply cut the hose.

2 With a basin wrench, loosen the nut on the one or two mounting shanks. If there is a sprayer hose guide, loosen it from underneath with a basin wrench as well. On other types of faucets, you may need to loosen a center mounting nut.

ONE-HANDLE INSTALLATION

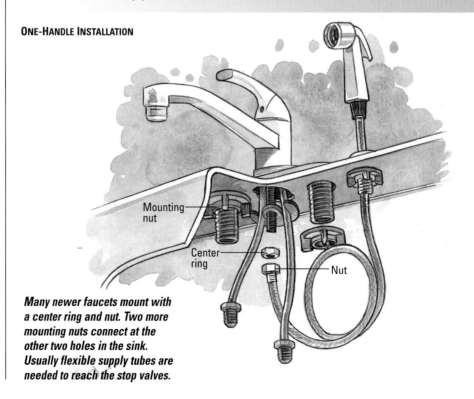

Many newer faucets mount with a center ring and nut. Two more mounting nuts connect at the other two holes in the sink. Usually flexible supply tubes are needed to reach the stop valves.

3 Lift out the old faucet. If you feel resistance, check underneath to make sure everything has been disconnected. In rare cases, an old faucet will have supply tubes that are sweated on. See *page 98* for how to cut away the old supply tubes.

Putty rope

4 If the faucet does not have a rubber gasket, roll out a rope of plumber's putty and press it into place on the bottom of the new faucet. Make sure it is thick enough at all points to completely seal the faucet body.

Mounting nut

Base of sprayer support

Sprayer hose

Center faucet hole

5 If you have a sprayer, install the sprayer support, tightening the mounting nut first by hand, then with a basin wrench. Don't overtighten. Run the sprayer hose through the sprayer support and through the center faucet hole.

Center mounting nut

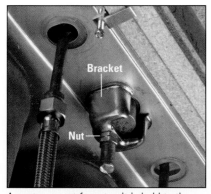

Bracket

Nut

A center-mount faucet unit is held to the sink with a single bracket instead of two tailpieces doubling as hot and cold supplies. Typically, a bracket is snugged up against the sink with a nut. With center mounts, supply tubes can be installed before the faucet is set into the sink.

WHAT IF...
The faucet has a gasket?

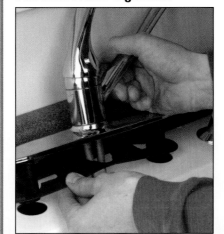

Some faucets have a rubber gasket, so they do not need a rope of putty. Make sure that the gasket is centered before tightening the mounting nuts.

STANLEY PRO TIP

Cleaning a gunky deck

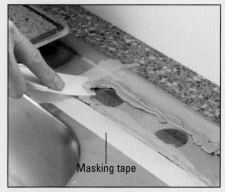

Masking tape

If the sink deck is caked with old putty, clean it before installing the new faucet. Place masking tape where the faucet will not cover and scrape with a plastic putty knife. Clean the surface with an abrasive pad and mineral spirits or alcohol.

Installing a kitchen faucet (continued)

Sprayer hose

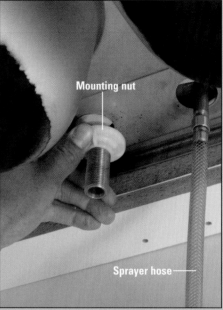

Mounting nut

Sprayer hose

6 Attach as many things as possible before installing the faucet, to minimize the work under the sink. In this case, the sprayer tube can be attached; mounting nuts must be attached from underneath before supply tubes can be installed.

7 Slip the new faucet into place. If the faucet has inlets and a mounting nut in the center, getting all those tubes through the center hole will be a tight fit. Take care not to scratch the threads. If you need to bend a copper tube, do so gently to avoid kinking it.

8 Have a helper hold the faucet straight while you install the mounting nuts underneath. For this type, first apply the mounting nuts and tighten them finger-tight. Check that the faucet is mounted straight before tightening with a basin wrench.

SUPPLY TUBE OPTIONS

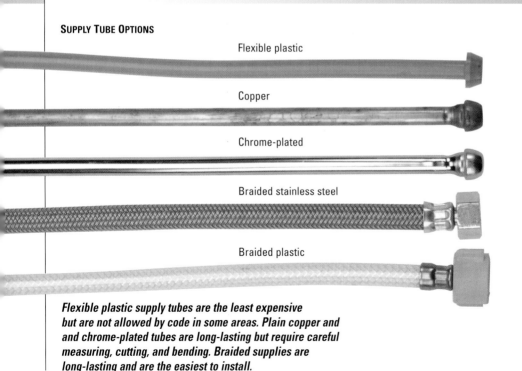

Flexible plastic

Copper

Chrome-plated

Braided stainless steel

Braided plastic

Flexible plastic supply tubes are the least expensive but are not allowed by code in some areas. Plain copper and and chrome-plated tubes are long-lasting but require careful measuring, cutting, and bending. Braided supplies are long-lasting and are the easiest to install.

WHAT IF...
Copper runs to stop valves?

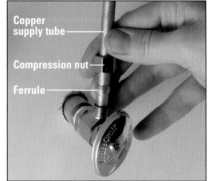

Copper supply tube

Compression nut

Ferrule

Many plumbers prefer to install copper or chrome-plated copper supply tubes rather than flexible lines. This saves a bit of money and makes for a slightly more solid installation. Cut the supply tubes with a tubing cutter (pages 98, 109), and bend them with a tubing bender (page 99). Attach the compression fitting (page 100).

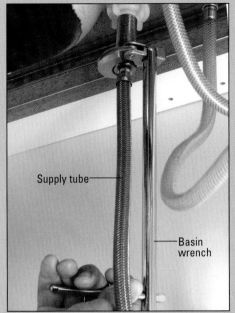

Supply tube

Basin wrench

9 Fasten each supply tube by hand to the faucet base. Then tighten the connection using a basin wrench.

10 Screw on and tighten the supply tubes to the stop valves. Use two wrenches or pliers to prevent bending the pipes connected to the stop valves.

11 If you bumped the drain trap while working, you may have loosened its joints. To check, fill the sinks with water, remove the stoppers, and watch for any leaks. Tighten leaky joints.

PULLOUT FAUCET INSTALLATION

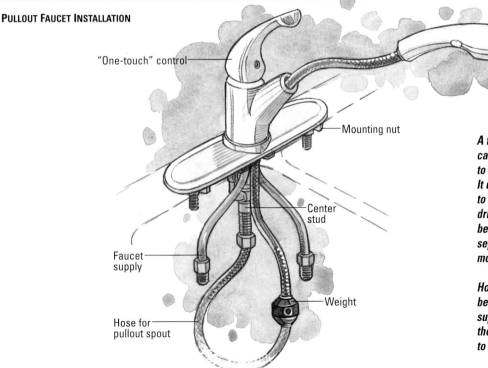

"One-touch" control

Pullout spout

Mounting nut

Center stud

Faucet supply

Weight

Hose for pullout spout

A faucet with a pullout spout, sometimes called a "one-touch" faucet, makes it easy to switch from standard faucet to sprayer. It uses only three sink holes, freeing one up to accommodate a hot-water dispenser or a drinking-water faucet. Most pullout spouts are better built than standard kitchen faucets with separate sprayers, so the sprayer feature is more reliable.

Installation is similar to a standard faucet. However, it is important that the sprayer hose be free to move without becoming entangled in supply or drain lines. To install the faucet, slide the weight onto the hose, and connect the hose to the center stud of the faucet.

INSTALLING A BATHROOM FAUCET

Like a kitchen sink, a bathroom sink typically has three holes, but they are spaced closer together. Installation is similar to a kitchen faucet, with the added complication of a pop-up stopper assembly.

Unless you have a wall-hung sink with no cabinet or pedestal below, the work space under a bathroom sink can be cramped. If you have a pedestal sink, check to see whether the bowl is securely attached to a wall bracket. If so, you can remove the pedestal while you work *(pages 74–75)*. If you have a vanity sink with a cabinet below, it may be easier to detach the trap, remove the sink, and install the faucet with the sink on top of sawhorses.

If there are no stop valves under the sink, install them before putting in the new sink *(pages 110–111)*.

Whether you reuse the old supply tubes or buy new ones, make sure they are long enough to reach the stop valves. Purchase fittings (either ⅜- or ½-inch) that will fit your stop valves.

PRESTART CHECKLIST

☐ **TIME**
About 2 hours to install a bathroom faucet with a pop-up drain assembly

☐ **TOOLS**
Screwdriver, adjustable wrench, putty knife, groove-joint pliers, basin wrench

☐ **SKILLS**
Shutting off water, working under a sink, attaching plumbing parts

☐ **PREP**
Shut off the water to the old faucet. If the drain trap is in the way, you may have to remove it.

☐ **MATERIALS**
New faucet, new pop-up drain (usually comes with the faucet), plumber's putty, perhaps supply tubes

1 **Shut off the water.** From below, disconnect the supply tubes and the mounting nuts from the stop valves. Loosen the setscrew that holds the clevis strap to the lifter rod, pinch the spring clip, and slide the clevis strap off the pivot rod.

2 Pull out the old faucet and clean the sink *(pages 60–61)*. You may be able to connect the supply tubes to the faucet, using two wrenches. If no rubber gasket is provided, press a rope of putty to the sink deck or to the underside of the faucet body. Lower the faucet into place.

TWO TYPES OF BATHROOM FAUCETS

A single-handle faucet (left) usually has copper supply tubes in the center and a mounting nut on each side. On a two-handle unit (right), the mounting nuts are below the handles.

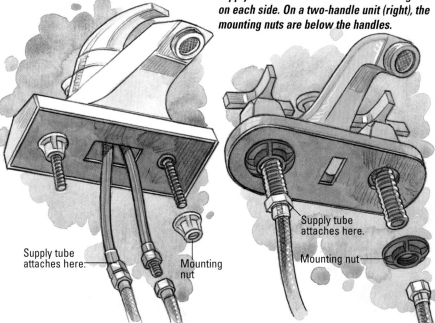

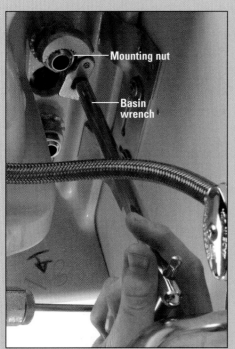

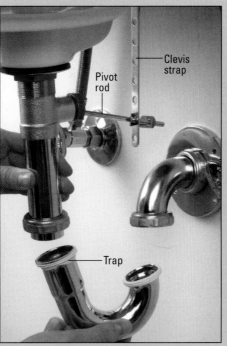

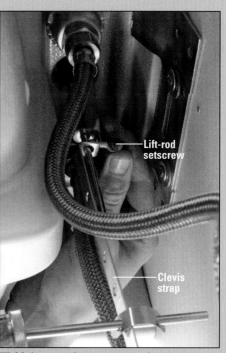

3 Have a helper hold the faucet straight while you tighten mounting nuts from below. If the faucet is not solidly attached after hand-tightening, use a basin wrench to tighten the nuts further.

4 You can use the existing drain body, or install a new one. With the stopper closed all the way, slide the clevis strap onto the lift rod and the pivot rod, using the spring clip to hold it in place. Tighten the setscrew that holds the strap to the lift rod. Install the trap *(pages 24–25)*.

5 Make sure the stopper seals water when the lift rod is pulled up and that it opens fully when the rod is pushed down. To adjust, loosen the setscrew and move the clevis strap up or down.

Installing a drain body

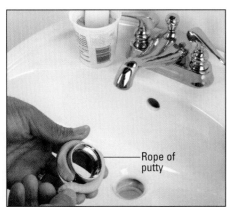

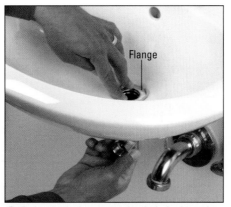

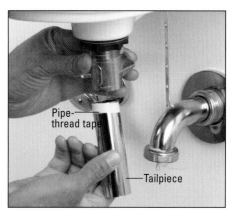

1 Loosen the slip nut to disconnect the drain body from the trap. Remove the locknut under the sink, and slide out the old drain body. Clean away caked-on putty. Place new rope of putty around the hole, slip the new drain flange through the hole, and press it into place.

2 Twist the locknut onto the drain body, and slip on the friction washer and the rubber gasket. Hold the flange with one hand while you hand screw the drain body into it. Tighten the locknut with groove-joint pliers, taking care that the drain body faces rear.

3 Install the pivot rod, and install the clevis strap (see Step 4). Apply pipe-thread tape to the threaded end of the tailpiece, and screw it onto the drain body. Install the trap *(pages 24–25)*.

Installing Sinks & Appliances

That old sink may seem like a permanent part of your home, but replacing it is easier than you think. In most cases, an attractive new sink can be found to fit the hole left by the old sink, or the old spot can be easily enlarged to make room for a more spacious sink.

This chapter provides detailed instructions for installing popular types of bathroom and kitchen sinks. For the bathroom, you can choose a vanity sink with a cabinet below or a stylish pedestal sink. For the kitchen, choose self-rimming, flush-mounted, or underhung sinks made of stainless steel, enameled cast iron, or acrylic (see *page 69*).

Plumbing a new sink

If the new sink has holes in the same place as the old one, reattaching the trap will be a simple job. However, if the new sink is shaped differently, or if you will be adding a garbage disposer, you will need to install a new trap and drain.

Installing the drain for a bathroom sink (which uses 1¼-inch pipe) is usually simple, once the pop-up assembly has been installed. It must have a P or S trap, and the drain should attach to a threaded pipe in the wall or in the floor.

The job of installing a kitchen sink (which uses 1½-inch pipe) gets more complicated, especially if it has two bowls. Fortunately kits are available with all the parts you need.

If you encounter an obstacle or unusual situation, make a drawing or photo of it and ask a home center or hardware store salesperson for advice. Usually an extension and an elbow with slip nuts and washers are all you need. Take your time to ensure that the pieces fit; if you have to force a joint, it will likely leak.

Sink appliances

A garbage disposer is an indispensible part of a modern kitchen. For only a couple hours of work and a small investment, you can also add a hot-water dispenser or a water filter. A dishwasher is surprisingly easy to install.

A sink, disposer, hot-water dispenser, and even a dishwasher are surprisingly easy to install.

Chapter Preview

Installing a kitchen sink
page 68

Installing a bathroom vanity
page 72

Installing a pedestal sink
page 74

Setting up a laundry room
page 76

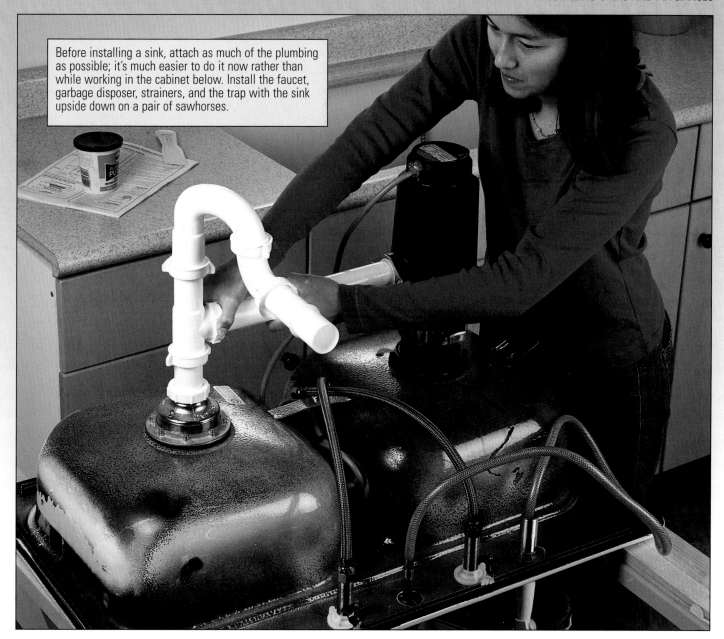

Before installing a sink, attach as much of the plumbing as possible; it's much easier to do it now rather than while working in the cabinet below. Install the faucet, garbage disposer, strainers, and the trap with the sink upside down on a pair of sawhorses.

Installing a garbage disposer
page 78

Adding a hot-water dispenser
page 80

Adding an under-sink filter
page 82

Hooking up an ice maker
page 83

Replacing a dishwasher
page 84

INSTALLING A KITCHEN SINK

If the new sink is the same size and depth as the old one, replacing it will be a matter of disconnecting and reattaching fittings. If the sink is a different size or if you are installing a new countertop, additional planning is required.

The countertop and the sink

The steps on the following four pages describe how to install a self-rimming stainless-steel sink, one of the most common types. A self-rimming cast-iron or acrylic sink is actually easier to install *(page 70).*

The following steps show how to install a sink in a laminate countertop. If the countertop will be tiled, cut a hole in the substrate, check to make sure the sink fits, then lay the tiles before installing the sink.

PRESTART CHECKLIST

☐ **TIME**
Most of a day to cut a hole in a countertop, install a sink, and connect the plumbing

☐ **TOOLS**
Drill, saber saw, tape measure, screwdriver, caulk gun, adjustable wrench, groove-joint pliers, spud wrench

☐ **SKILLS**
Cutting a countertop, connecting a P trap, installing a faucet

☐ **PREP**
Shut off water to the old sink. Choose a sink that fits in the cabinet and set it on a pair of sawhorses.

☐ **MATERIALS**
Sink, plumber's putty or silicone caulk, faucet, garbage disposer, supply tubes, trap materials to suit your situation (for instance, a double-bowl trap kit)

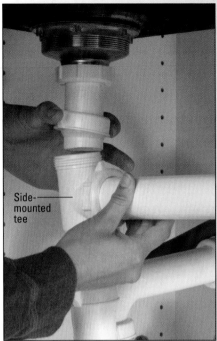

Side-mounted tee

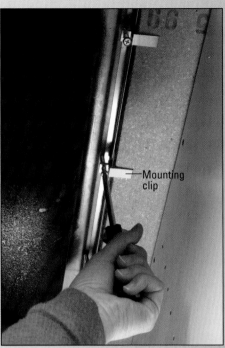

Mounting clip

1 **Shut off the water** and open the faucet until water stops flowing. Disconnect the old faucet's supply tubes *(page 60)* and disconnect the trap at one point at least. If there is a dishwasher hose attached to the drain or disposer, unscrew or squeeze the hose clamp and pull off the hose.

2 If the old sink is stainless steel or rimmed cast iron, loosen the mounting clips underneath and turn them sideways so they won't be in the way when you pull out the sink. If the old sink is cast iron or acrylic, use a utility knife to cut the bead of caulk that holds the sink to the countertop.

TYPICAL DRAIN CONNECTIONS

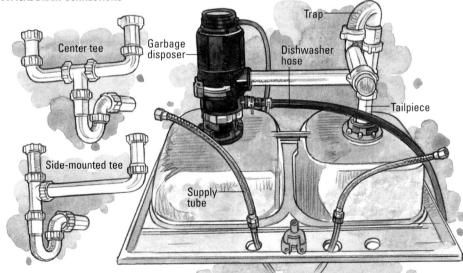

Center tee · Garbage disposer · Trap · Dishwasher hose · Tailpiece · Side-mounted tee · Supply tube

A typical double-bowl installation with garbage disposer and dishwasher hose has a single trap below the nondisposer sink. If there is no garbage disposer, use either a center- or side-mounted tee, depending on the location of the drain line.

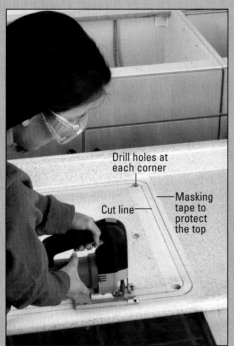

Drill holes at each corner

Masking tape to protect the top

Cut line

Spud wrench

3 If you are installing a new countertop or if the new sink is larger than the old one, place the new sink upside down on top of the countertop, positioned over the opening in the cabinet below. Trace around the sink, then draw another line ¾ inch inside the first line. Cut along the second line.

4 With the sink upside down on a pair of sawhorses, install the strainers (see *pages 34–35* for complete instructions). A garbage disposer has its own special strainer. Make sure you know to which bowl the disposer will be attached.

5 Install the disposer *(pages 78–79)* and as much of the trap as is feasible. For this installation, a kit supplies all the parts for a double-bowl sink with disposer. Temporarily set the sink in the hole to see if the pipes line up with the drain line that leads to the wall or floor.

Choosing a sink

When it comes to sink materials, you generally get what you pay for. An inexpensive stainless-steel sink (top) flexes when you push on it, scratches easily, and is difficult to keep clean. A higher-quality 6- or 8-gauge stainless-steel sink, such as one with a burnished finish (right), is a better choice. When choosing a stainless-steel sink, make sure the underside is well coated with sound-deadening insulation.

An enameled cast-iron sink (right) comes in a variety of colors and lasts much longer than an enameled-steel sink. Acrylic sinks like the one shown (bottom right) have the look of enameled cast iron, and the higher-end models are nearly as durable. Both cast-iron and acrylic sinks have insulating properties that keep water warm in them longer than in a stainless-steel sink.

Stainless steel

Heavy-gauge stainless steel

Cast iron

Acrylic

STANLEY PRO TIP

Assembling a trap

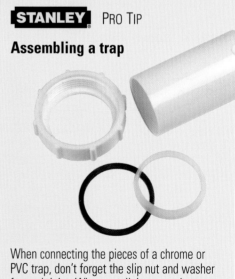

When connecting the pieces of a chrome or PVC trap, don't forget the slip nut and washer for each joint. Where a tailpiece attaches to a strainer, a special type of washer may be used. You'll probably need to cut at least one pipe; use a hacksaw or a fine-toothed saw (for PVC only). See *pages 24–25* for more instructions.

Installing a kitchen sink *(continued)*

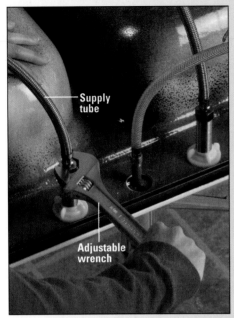

Supply
tube

Adjustable
wrench

Clips face
sideways, so
the sink slips
into the hole.

Putty

6 Install the faucet *(pages 60–63* for complete instructions). Hold the faucet straight and centered over the holes as you tighten the mounting nuts. Attach supply tubes to the faucet inlets.

7 Temporarily set the sink in the hole and make sure the drain trap lines up with the pipe in the wall and that the supply tubes reach the stop valves. Return the sink to the sawhorses and slide several mounting clips onto each flange. Use a bit of plumber's putty to hold each clip sideways.

8 Roll out a rope of plumber's putty and press it all around the sink flange. Build it up slightly higher than the flange at all points, so it will seal completely. An alternative method is to apply a bead of silicone caulk.

REFRESHER COURSE
Installing faucets

Rubber
gasket

A kitchen faucet uses three holes in the sink; a sprayer unit may go in the fourth hole. Take care not to bend copper inlets while attaching the supply tubes. Set the faucet body in a rope of plumber's putty or use a rubber gasket. (See *pages 60–63*.)

WHAT IF...
You are installing a cast-iron sink?

A cast-iron sink is very heavy, so have someone help you lift and position it. Its weight actually makes it easier to install than a stainless-steel sink, because it requires no clips.

Once you make sure the sink fits in the hole and that the plumbing lines up underneath, remove the sink and apply a bead of silicone caulk around the hole. Carefully lower the sink into the hole. Avoid sliding it, which could compromise the caulk seal. Press down gently. If caulk oozes out at every point around the rim, you know that the seal is complete. Scrape away excess caulk with a plastic or wood scraper. Allow the caulk to set for several hours before attaching the plumbing.

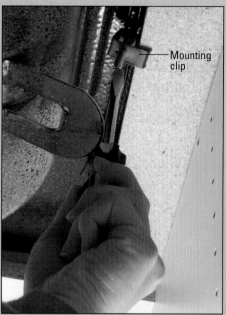

9 With a helper, carefully lower the sink into the hole. If any putty falls out, replace it; the seal has to completely surround the flange. Press down all around the sink so that putty starts to ooze out at every point. Scrape off the excess with a plastic putty knife.

10 From underneath, turn the clips so they grab the underside of the countertop. There should be a clip every 8 inches. Tighten each clip with a screwdriver or a drill equipped with a screwdriver bit.

11 Attach the trap to the pipe that leads to the house drain. Tighten all the connections with groove-joint pliers. To test for leaks, fill each bowl with water, then remove the stopper and watch for drips. Run the disposer with the water on and check for drips.

FLUSH-MOUNTED AND UNDERMOUNTED SINKS

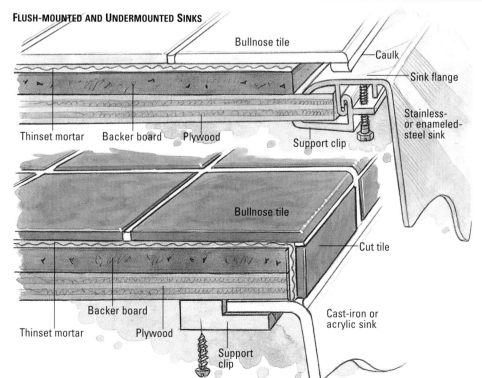

Many people dislike self-rimming sinks because crumbs and dirt tend to collect around the rim. A flush-mounted or underhung sink makes for easier cleaning but requires special countertop treatments.

Install a flush-mounted sink with its rim resting on the plywood substrate. Then install concrete backer board around the sink. Finally place the tiles so they partially overlap the sink flange. Grout the tiles and add a bead of caulk along the sink flange

An underhung sink can be installed and plumbed after the substrate is installed. Then install the tiles as shown, with thin vertical pieces around the perimeter and bullnose trim pieces overlapping them.

For the ultimate in "wipeability," consider a solid-surface countertop with an integrated sink. This type of installation is usually done by professionals with special equipment.

INSTALLING A BATHROOM VANITY SINK

Installing a bathroom sink in a vanity is simplified by the fact that the supply lines and the drain are all hidden within a cabinet. If the cabinet has no back, simply attach it to the wall so it encloses the plumbing. However, if the cabinet has a back, measure and cut three holes for the two supply lines and the drain.

Choosing a cabinet and top

A high-quality vanity cabinet is made of hardwood to resist water damage. A less expensive cabinet made of laminated particleboard will quickly disintegrate if it gets wet.

A vanity top typically is a single piece comprised of the bowl, countertop, and backsplash. Acrylic or plastic vanity tops are inexpensive, but they scratch and stain more easily than other materials.

PRESTART CHECKLIST

☐ **TIME**
Two to three hours to install a basic cabinet and vanity top with faucet

☐ **TOOLS**
Drill, hammer, screwdriver, level, adjustable wrench, groove-joint pliers, basin wrench

☐ **SKILLS**
Installing a faucet, attaching a P trap, connecting supply tubes, simple carpentry

☐ **PREP**
Shut off the water and remove the old sink.

☐ **MATERIALS**
Vanity cabinet and top, faucet, P trap, supply tubes that fit the stop valves, plumber's putty, wood shims, screws

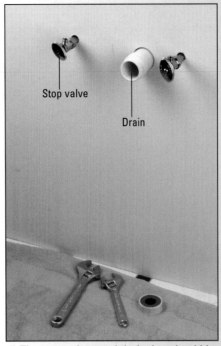

1 The stop valves and drainpipe should be in place and close enough together to be enclosed by the cabinet. If your vanity cabinet has a back (many do not), remove the handles from the stop valves. Then measure and cut holes for the drain and the two supply pipes.

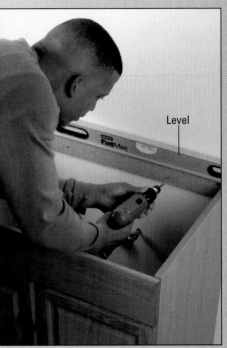

2 Slide the cabinet into place and check it for level in both directions. If necessary, slip shims under the bottom or behind the back of the cabinet. Drive screws through the cabinet framing into wall studs to secure the cabinet.

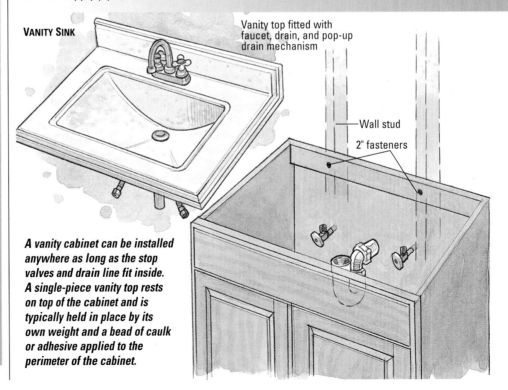

VANITY SINK

Vanity top fitted with faucet, drain, and pop-up drain mechanism

Wall stud

2" fasteners

A vanity cabinet can be installed anywhere as long as the stop valves and drain line fit inside. A single-piece vanity top rests on top of the cabinet and is typically held in place by its own weight and a bead of caulk or adhesive applied to the perimeter of the cabinet.

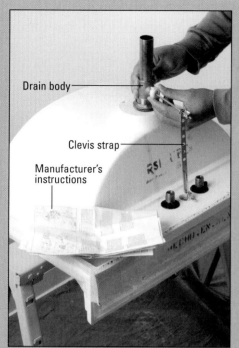

Drain body

Clevis strap

Manufacturer's instructions

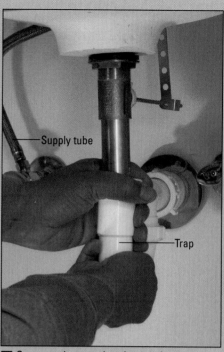

Supply tube

Trap

3 Set the vanity top upside down on a pair of sawhorses and install the plumbing. See *pages 64–65* for installing the faucet, drain body, and pop-up assembly. Check the manufacturer's instructions for specific details.

4 Set the top onto the cabinet and check that it is centered. Remove it, apply caulk or adhesive along the top edge of the vanity, and reinstall the top.

5 Connect the supply tubes to the stop valves. Connect the trap *(pages 24–25).*

Installing a drop-in sink

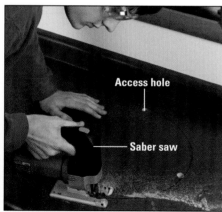

Access hole

Saber saw

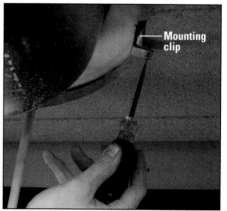

Mounting clip

1 To install a drop-in self-rimming sink, first install a laminate countertop, or for a tile countertop, plywood and concrete backer board. Use the template if provided, or turn the sink upside down on the counter and trace its outline. Draw a line ¾ inch inside the first line. Cut this second line with a saber saw.

2 Plumb the sink (Step 3 above). Apply a bead of bathtub caulk or a rope of plumber's putty around the hole and set the sink. If the sink doesn't have mounting clips, apply a bead of silicone caulk instead of putty. Set the sink in, wipe away the excess caulk, and wait several hours before attaching the plumbing.

3 If your sink has mounting clips, slip several of them in place and turn them sideways so they grab the underside of the counter. Tighten the screws. Attach the supply lines and the drain trap.

INSTALLING A PEDESTAL SINK

A pedestal sink saves space in a bathroom but requires strong support from the wall, which often means adding extra framing.

Installing the framing and patching the wall will take more time than the plumbing. The project will probably require several days: On the first day, install the framing and patch the wall. On the second day, finish the patching and paint the wall. Install the sink on the third day. (If you have a tiled wall, consider installing the framing by cutting into the wall in the room behind the sink location.)

An inexpensive pedestal sink may actually rest on the pedestal—an arrangement that makes the plumbing installation difficult and future repairs nearly impossible. Buy a sink that mounts on a bracket; the pedestal is for looks only.

If your supply lines are close together, you may be able to hide them behind the pedestal. Otherwise, let the plumbing show.

PRESTART CHECKLIST

☐ **TIME**
About 5 hours of work spread over a period of three days (see above)

☐ **TOOLS**
Drill, hammer, drywall saw, taping knife, sanding block, paintbrush, screwdriver, adjustable wrench, groove-joint pliers

☐ **SKILLS**
Installing a bathroom faucet with pop-up drain, connecting a trap, cutting drywall

☐ **PREP**
Locate studs behind the wall near the plumbing.

☐ **MATERIALS**
Pedestal sink, bathroom faucet, supply tubes that fit the stop valves, plumber's putty, 2×6 or 2×8 piece, screws, drywall, joint compound, drywall tape, paint

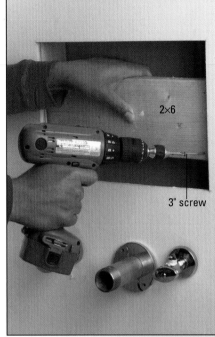

1 Measure and mark the bracket height. To support the bracket, cut a hole in the wall that spans two studs. Cut a piece of 2×6 or 2×8 to fit between the studs and attach it with screws. Drive the screws at an angle through the brace and into the studs.

2 Cut a piece of drywall to fit and attach it to the brace with screws. Smooth pieces of drywall tape around the edges. Use a taping blade to cover the tape with joint compound. Allow the compound to dry, then sand until the patch is smooth. Paint the patch.

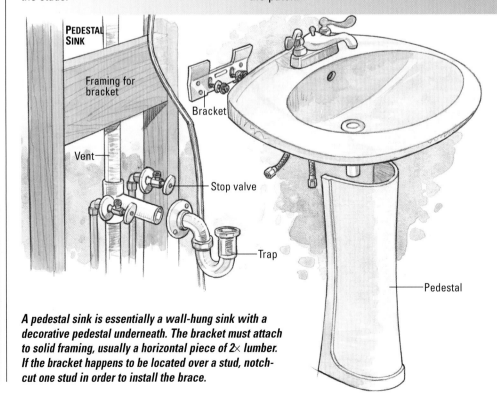

A pedestal sink is essentially a wall-hung sink with a decorative pedestal underneath. The bracket must attach to solid framing, usually a horizontal piece of 2× lumber. If the bracket happens to be located over a stud, notch-cut one stud in order to install the brace.

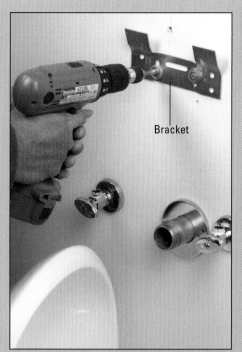

Bracket

3 Set the sink on top of the pedestal and against the wall. Hold the bracket in place and mark the position of the bracket. Install the bracket by driving screws through the wall into the 2× brace.

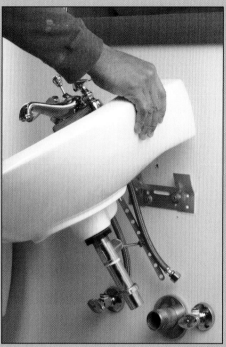

4 Install the faucet and the drain body on the sink *(pages 64–65)*. Lower the sink onto the bracket. Slide the pedestal in place to make sure the bracket is at the right height and adjust it, if necessary. Hook the supply tubes to the stop valves and attach the drain.

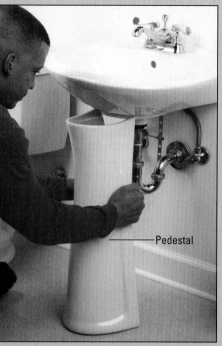

Pedestal

5 Slide the pedestal under the sink. Stand back to determine if the pedestal looks level and sits squarely on the floor. Adjust it as needed. You may caulk the bottom of the pedestal or leave it uncaulked so it can be removed for cleaning.

Decorative plumbing

Most pedestals are too narrow to hide the stop valves and supply tubes, so install attractive plumbing. Decorative stop valves are available in brass finish or old-fashioned ceramic handles, and supply tubes come in solid copper tubing or braided chrome.

STANLEY PRO TIP

Support the trap

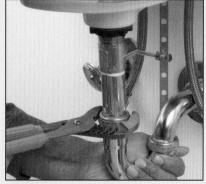

Trap joints are fragile. While tightening one joint, it's easy to strain another. The result can be a persistent leak. When tightening a joint, always support the adjacent section of pipe.

WHAT IF...
You have a bolt-down pedestal?

Lag screw

Some pedestals are designed to be bolted to the floor. Tighten the bolts until snug; any tighter and the pedestal might crack.

SETTING UP A LAUNDRY ROOM

A washing machine needs hot and cold water and a place for the water to drain. Hot and cold water must be brought to within a couple of feet of a washing machine. Install washing machine valves, which look like outdoor hose bibs but point straight down.

The washer drain hose hooks to a sink or a standpipe. The drain for either of these must slope downward at a rate of ¼ inch per running foot.

Many washing machines are self-leveling. Grab the machine by its control panel at the top rear, pull forward to slightly tilt the machine, and let it drop back solidly on all four feet. Adjust the front legs to make sure the machine is level in both directions.

PRESTART CHECKLIST

☐ **TIME**
About half a day

☐ **TOOLS**
Screwdriver, groove-joint pliers, propane torch, hacksaw, tubing cutter

☐ **SKILLS**
Working with copper and PVC pipe

☐ **PREP**
Locate the nearest supply and drain lines.

☐ **MATERIALS**
Utility sink, washing machine with drain hose, solder, flux, PVC primer and glue, 1½-inch trap, pipes and fittings, masonry screws

Mini tubing cutter

1 **Shut off water** to the supply pipes and drain the lines. To tap into a copper supply pipe, cut the pipe with a tubing cutter where you plan to install a tee fitting.

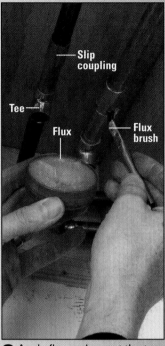

Slip coupling

Tee

Flux

Flux brush

2 Apply flux and sweat the tee fitting in place (see *pages 98–101*). If there is not enough movement in the pipe, a piece of pipe and a slip coupling (shown above) may be necessary. Or try a compression fitting *(page 100)*.

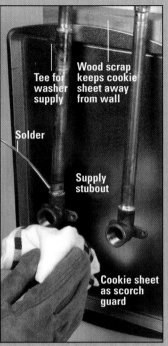

Tee for washer supply

Wood scrap keeps cookie sheet away from wall

Solder

Supply stubout

Cookie sheet as scorch guard

3 Add lengths of pipe to reach the laundry tub, including tees to run pipes to the washer. At the end of each supply pipe, sweat on a brass supply stubout. Anchor the stubouts to the wall with masonry screws.

LAUNDRY ROOM OVERVIEW

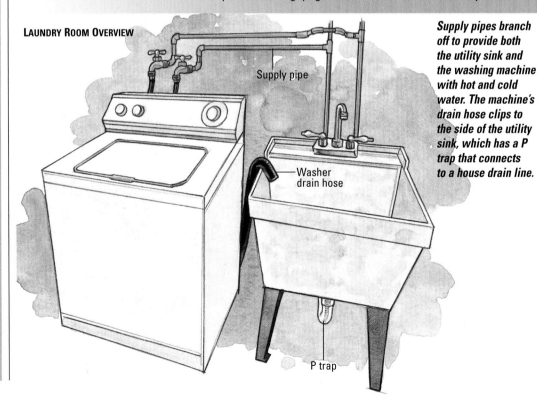

Supply pipe

Washer drain hose

P trap

Supply pipes branch off to provide both the utility sink and the washing machine with hot and cold water. The machine's drain hose clips to the side of the utility sink, which has a P trap that connects to a house drain line.

Elbow

Hose bib

Supply stubout

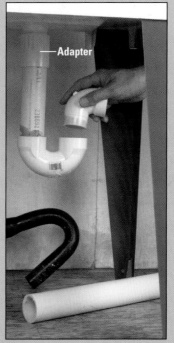

Adapter

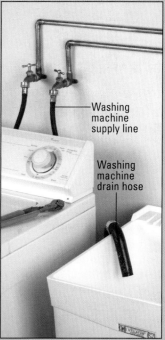

Washing machine supply line

Washing machine drain hose

4 Run copper lines to the washer. Add supply stubouts and anchor them to the wall with masonry screws. Apply pipe-thread tape and hand twist each hose bib into its stubout; then tighten it with a wrench.

5 Install stop valves *(pages 110–111)* on the sink stubouts. A plastic utility sink is inexpensive and easy to assemble. Install a faucet onto the sink and connect supply tubes to the stop valves.

6 To work with PVC drainpipe, see *pages 102–103*. Tap into a drain line with a tee fitting, and run a drainpipe (sloped at $\frac{1}{4}$ inch per running foot) to the sink. Glue an adapter to the pipe end and attach the trap.

7 Set the washing machine in place and level it. Screw the machine's supply lines to the valves and tighten with pliers. Drape the drain hose over the side of the utility sink and clamp it firmly in place.

WHAT IF...
You extend steel pipe?

To tap into galvanized steel lines, cut and remove a section of pipe. Replace the section with a combination of lengths of threaded pipe, nipples, a tee fitting, and a union to suit your situation. Extend the supply line from the tee and attach a stop valve. (See *pages 104–105* for working with steel pipe.)

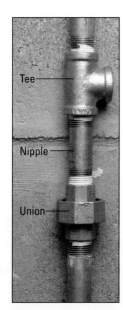

Tee

Nipple

Union

Making a direct drain connection

Where there is no room for a utility sink, install a standpipe for the drain. The pipe must be large enough to insert the washing machine's drain hose into it, and it must rise above the top of the machine's water level.

Washing machine supply box

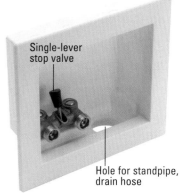

Single-lever stop valve

Hole for standpipe, drain hose

If your walls are not finished (the studs are exposed), or if you are able to run pipes through walls, consider installing a washing-machine supply box, which can be recessed into the wall for a neater look. It controls both hot and cold water with one valve and provides an outlet for a drain hose.

INSTALLING A GARBAGE DISPOSER

Replacing an existing disposer with one of the same size is simply a matter of disconnecting and reconnecting fittings. However, if there is no existing disposer, or if the new unit is a different size, you will need to reconfigure your sink trap.

A disposer must be plugged into an GFCI (ground-fault circuit interrupter) receptacle or directly wired to a junction box that is controlled by a switch. The switch is typically on the wall above the countertop. If the wiring does not exist under your sink, have an electrician do this work for you.

Local codes may regulate the use of disposers. In some areas they are banned because they add to the sewage load. Codes may require that a dishwasher drain hose be routed through an air gap before entering a disposer *(page 84)*.

Installation, parts, and procedures vary considerably among disposer models. Follow the manufacturer's directions.

PRESTART CHECKLIST

☐ **TIME**
Between one and three hours, depending on changes to plumbing

☐ **TOOLS**
Screwdriver, groove-joint pliers, wire strippers

☐ **SKILLS**
Making simple electrical splices, installing a basket strainer

☐ **PREP**
Remove an existing disposer or part of the trap, and the strainer as well.

☐ **MATERIALS**
Garbage disposer, wire nuts, appliance cord (thicker than normal extension cord) or armored cable ("whip"), trap parts

1 Remove the electrical cover plate from the bottom of the disposer. Install a cable clamp and run an appliance cord through it. Strip the wire ends and splice the wires—black to black, white to white, ground (green) to ground. Cap each splice with a wire nut. Replace the cover plate.

2 Remove the old strainer *(pages 34–35)* and clean the area around the hole. Press a rope of plumber's putty around the underside of the disposer sink flange. Press the flange into place. Have a helper hold the flange in position while you perform the next step from below.

GARBAGE DISPOSER INSTALLATION

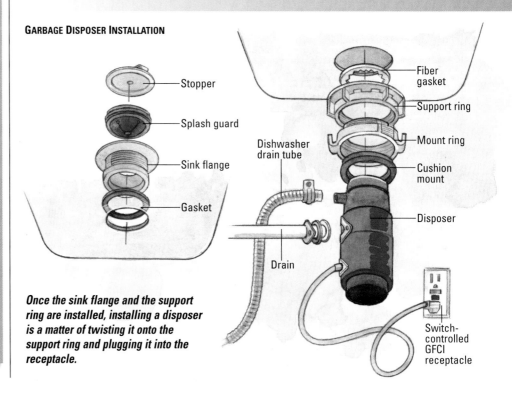

Once the sink flange and the support ring are installed, installing a disposer is a matter of twisting it onto the support ring and plugging it into the receptacle.

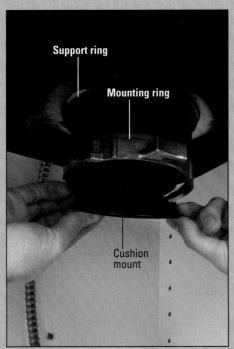

Support ring

Mounting ring

Cushion
mount

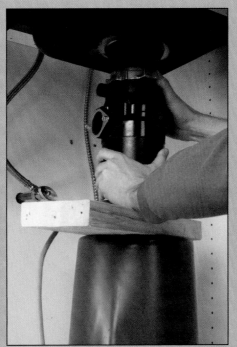

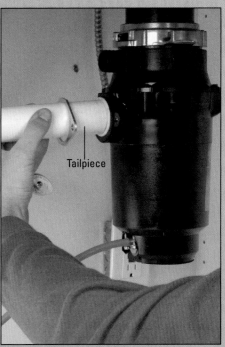

Tailpiece

3 To install this type of mounting ring, slip on the fiber gasket and hand tighten the support ring. Slide the mount ring over the flange and install the cushion mount, making sure the groove on the inside fits over the lip of the sink flange. Scrape out any excess putty on the inside of the sink.

4 If the disposer is not too heavy and you can get into a comfortable position, simply lift the disposer up onto the mounting ring and twist it so it catches and is firmly anchored. If you have trouble doing this, construct a simple platform to help support the disposer.

5 To connect to the drain line, either use the black elbow that comes with the disposer or discard the elbow and install a horizontal tailpiece, as shown. See *pages 24–25* for tips on assembling a trap.

Attaching a dishwasher

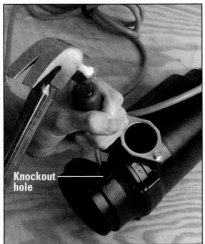

Knockout
hole

If you have a dishwasher, run its drain hose first to an air gap, then to the disposer's drain connection *(page 84)*. Use a hose clamp to hold the hose firm.

USE THE BLACK ELBOW
Other disposer drain options

Double bowl
installation

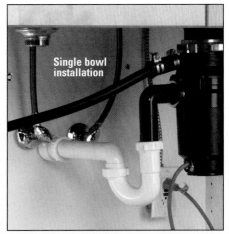

Single bowl
installation

Some local codes require that the drain line turn downward as soon as it leaves the disposer. Most disposers come with a black elbow designed to make this turn.

If you have a single-bowl sink, install the black elbow that comes with the disposer and run the drain line directly into a trap.

ADDING A HOT-WATER DISPENSER

This handy appliance delivers water that's about 200° F to the countertop. It plugs into a standard electrical receptacle. Small copper tubes run from a cold water line to the dispenser's tank, then up to a spout by the sink.

Installation tips

To install the dispenser, you must have an electrical receptacle that is always energized (not switched on or off) near the sink. To supply a garbage disposer and a hot-water dispenser from a single receptacle, have an electrician install a "split" GFCI receptacle.

Position the tank and the copper lines out of the way under the sink. Usually, the rear wall is preferable to a side wall.

You can screw a saddle-tee valve into the pipe without shutting off the water to the pipe. However, the valve is liable to get clogged. For a more trouble-free installation, shut off the water and drill a hole first (as shown in Step 1).

PRESTART CHECKLIST

☐ **TIME**
If there is an existing electrical receptacle and an available knockout hole on the sink, about an hour

☐ **TOOLS**
Drill, adjustable wrench or small wrenches, groove-joint pliers, basin wrench, perhaps a hole saw

☐ **SKILLS**
Mounting a unit with screws, assembling appliance parts

☐ **PREP**
Clear out the cabinet below the sink, and shut off water to a cold-water line.

☐ **MATERIALS**
Hot-water dispenser, saddle-tee valve or stop valve

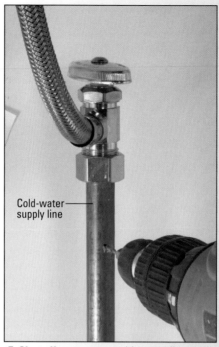

Cold-water supply line

1 **Shut off water** to a cold-water line and drain the line by running a faucet below. Check the manufacturer's instructions for drilling a hole the appropriate size (typically about ⅛ inch) for the saddle-tee valve needle. Squirt a little multipurpose oil on the bit before drilling.

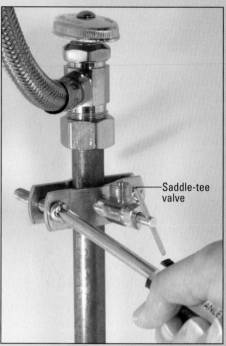

Saddle-tee valve

2 Position the two parts of a saddle-tee valve on the pipe, making sure the valve's point pokes into the hole. Tighten the screws. Turn the water back on and make sure the valve works and does not leak.

OVERVIEW OF HOT-WATER DISPENSER INSTALLATION

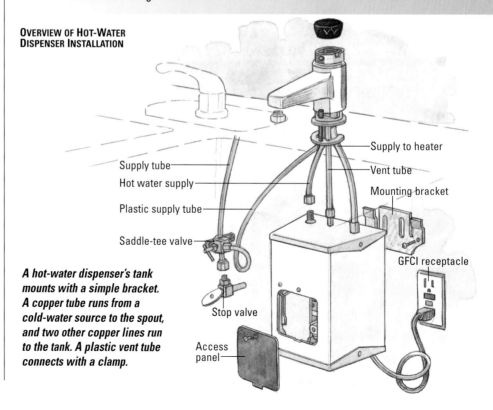

- Supply to heater
- Supply tube
- Vent tube
- Hot water supply
- Mounting bracket
- Plastic supply tube
- Saddle-tee valve
- GFCI receptacle
- Stop valve
- Access panel

A hot-water dispenser's tank mounts with a simple bracket. A copper tube runs from a cold-water source to the spout, and two other copper lines run to the tank. A plastic vent tube connects with a clamp.

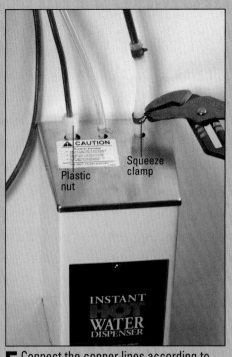

3 Mount the spout first. Carefully slip the copper lines through the knockout hole. Have a helper hold the spout in position while you work from underneath. Slide on the washer and the mounting nut. Tighten the nut by hand. If that is not firm enough, use a basin wrench to tighten it further.

4 Determine where the tank will go; the copper lines must be able to reach it. Install the bracket with screws, then slip the tank onto the bracket.

5 Connect the copper lines according to manufacturer's instructions. Bend the tubes carefully to avoid kinking; use a tubing bender to be safe *(page 99)*. Copper tubes connect to the tank using a plastic nut and ferrule; plastic tubes are secured with squeeze clamps.

Other water connections

For a more secure supply connection, install a tee fitting in the cold-water line and add a new stop valve.

Another method is to replace a standard stop valve with one that has two outlets, one for the faucet and one for the hot-water dispenser.

STANLEY PRO TIP

Maintaining a dispenser

Water that comes from this unit is nearly boiling, so keep small children away from the spout.

The tank gets hot, too, so keep paper bags and other flammables away from it.

If you expect not to use the dispenser for a few days, unplug it to save energy.

If the unit gets clogged, shut off the saddle-tee or stop valve and disconnect the supply line. Hold the line over a bucket and slowly turn the water back on. If flow is slow, the problem is probably the saddle-tee valve. Shut off the water and replace the valve.

If water drips from the spout when the unit is not in use, turn down the temperature. If that doesn't solve the problem, replace the spout.

No knockout on sink?

Drill a hole in a stainless-steel sink using a metal-cutting hole saw. In an acrylic sink, use a standard hole saw.

ADDING AN UNDER-SINK FILTER

A simple cabinet-mounted water filter can not only reduce the amount of sediment in water but also reduce water odor and improve its taste.

Local water conditions vary, so check with a salesperson at a home center or hardware store to see which filter will work best for you. Most carbon-based units make water more palatable.

If your water is excessively hard, have a water softener company install and perhaps maintain a water softener.

The unit shown here purifies all the cold water that runs through a kitchen faucet. Also available is a unit that has its own faucet for a separate source of filtered drinking water.

For an easy-to-install alternative, consider a faucet-mounted water filter. Some purify all the water flowing through the spout, while others have a separate valve that allows you to choose either filtered or unfiltered water. Both screw onto the faucet in place of the aerator.

PRESTART CHECKLIST

☐ **TIME**
An hour or two

☐ **TOOLS**
Drill, screwdriver, tubing cutter, adjustable wrench, groove-joint pliers

☐ **SKILLS**
Attaching with screws, cutting pipe, and making simple connections

☐ **PREP**
Add a tee and stop valve to the cold water supply; clear out the cabinet.

☐ **MATERIALS**
Water purifier, perhaps extra parts for connecting

Spout

Undersink mounting washer

1 Mount the spout to the knockout hole in the sink. Have a helper center the spout while you work below to tighten the mounting nut.

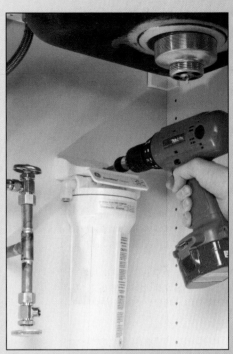

2 Shut off the water to the cold-water supply tube. Add a separate stop valve *(page 110–111)* or use one of the methods on *page 80–81*. Hold the filter in a convenient location and drive screws to attach it.

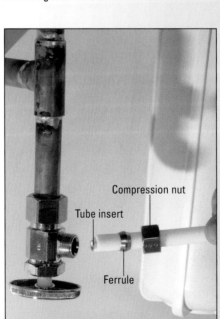

Compression nut

Tube insert

Ferrule

3 Trim to length the plastic supply tube for the filter. Poke the tube insert into the tube and slide on the compression nut and ferrule. Tighten the nut using a small adjustable wrench.

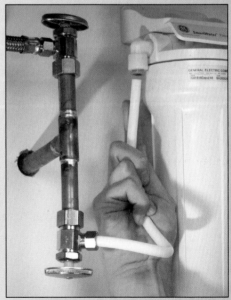

4 Connect the lines to the stop valve and spout, according to the manufacturer's instructions. Compression fittings make these connections easy. Water will now run through the filter before reaching the spout.

HOOKING UP AN ICE MAKER

Most new refrigerators have ice makers, but installation is typically an added expense. If you are retrofitting an ice maker to an older fridge, you will need to tap into a cold water line to supply the ice maker. In either case, doing it yourself is not difficult, as long as you work carefully with the copper tubing. If any kinks develop, don't try to "fix" them—cut them off or use a new piece of tubing.

For ice that tastes extra nice, install a water filter *(page 82)* and run the ice maker line through it.

As an alternative to the saddle-tee valve, install a new stop valve or a stop valve with two outlets *(page 81)*.

PRESTART CHECKLIST

☐ **TIME**
An hour or two for most installations

☐ **TOOLS**
Drill with long drill bit, adjustable wrench, screwdriver, tubing cutter, tubing bender

☐ **SKILLS**
Drilling holes, cutting and running copper tubing, making simple connections

☐ **PREP**
Locate a nearby cold-water pipe to tap.

☐ **MATERIALS**
Copper tubing, saddle-tee valve

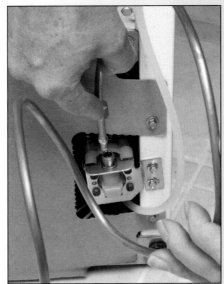

1 Behind the refrigerator, drill a hole through the floor to a basement or crawl space, or drill a horizontal hole to reach another room. Carefully unroll copper tubing and run it through the hole.

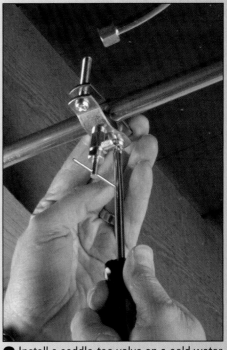

2 Install a saddle-tee valve on a cold water pipe *(page 80)* and hook the copper line to it by slipping on a ferrule and tightening a compression nut.

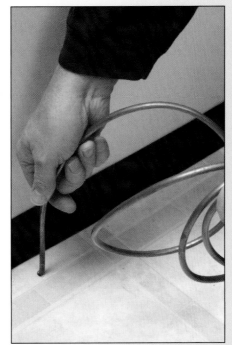

3 Leave enough slack in the copper line to allow you to slide out the refrigerator for cleaning. Connect the other end of the tubing to the ice maker connection on the refrigerator, using the same combination of a compression nut and a ferrule.

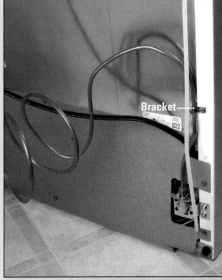

4 Moving the refrigerator for cleaning strains the compression fitting. Use one of the brackets provided with the refrigerator or the ice maker kit to firmly attach the copper tube to the fridge. Carefully bend the tubing into a coil as shown.

REPLACING A DISHWASHER

Though a dishwasher has the character of a major appliance and looks built-in, it's actually a simple job to remove an old dishwasher and install a new one.

If there is no existing dishwasher, you may need to call a professional to do the basic plumbing and electrical work. A dishwasher usually requires a 24-inch-wide space and fits between two base cabinets and under the countertop. Into that space must be run an electrical line (preferably using armored cable), a drain hose that connects to the garbage disposer or the trap under the sink, and a flexible copper supply line.

Some local codes require that the drain line run through an air gap mounted in a knockout hole in the sink. Other localities allow you to simply run the hose so that at some point it rises as high as the underside of the countertop.

PRESTART CHECKLIST

☐ **TIME**
Several hours to remove an existing dishwasher and install a replacement

☐ **TOOLS**
Drill, screwdriver, adjustable wrench, groove-joint pliers

☐ **SKILLS**
Making simple plumbing connections, attaching with screws

☐ **PREP**
Shut off the water to the dishwasher and turn off the electrical power at the service panel. Test to make sure both are off.

☐ **MATERIALS**
Dishwasher, drain hose, hose clamp, wire nuts, short screws

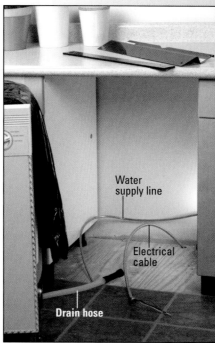

1 Shut off the water and the electrical power and test to make sure they are off. To remove an existing dishwasher, disconnect the electrical cable, drain, and water supply (reversing the work in Steps 3–5). Remove any mounting screws and slide out the unit.

2 Check that the two lines are long enough to reach the front of the opening. You may need to install a new drain line; clamp it to the garbage disposer drain opening or to an opening in a drain's tailpiece. Thread the drain line through the hole in the cabinet as you slide the dishwasher into place.

OVERALL SETUP FOR REPLACING A DISHWASHER

Three connections are needed for a dishwasher: An electrical cable supplies 120 volts of power; a drain line runs to the trap or garbage disposer, and a supply line that's hooked to a stop valve under the sink brings water to the dishwasher.

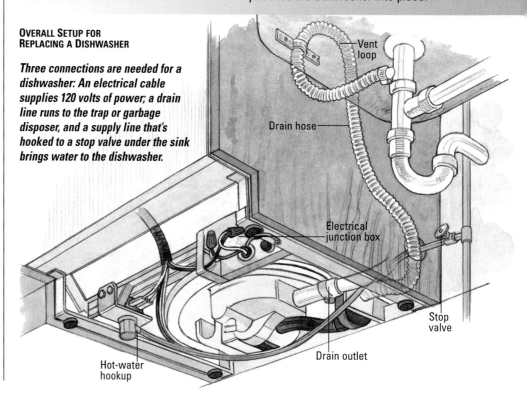

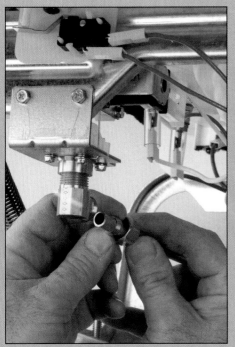

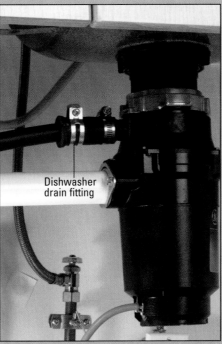

3 Slip a nut and ferrule onto the end of the supply line. Carefully bend the tubing and insert it into the supply inlet. Slide the ferrule down into the inlet and tighten the nut. Open the stop valve and check for leaks; you may need to tighten the compression nut further.

4 Run the drain line to the garbage disposer or a tailpiece with a special dishwasher drain fitting. Slide a hose clamp onto the hose, slip the hose onto the fitting, slide the clamp over the fitting, and tighten the clamp.

5 Run the electrical cable through the cable clamp and tighten the clamp nuts to hold the cable firm. Strip and splice wires—black to black, white to white, and ground (green) to ground. Cap each splice with a wire nut and install the electrical cover plate.

Anchor and level the dishwasher

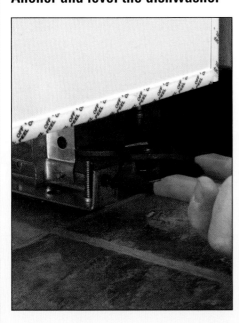

Slide the dishwasher far enough into its space so only its decorative trim is visible. If the dishwasher won't go in far enough, pull it out and look for obstructions.

Stand back and check that the dishwasher looks straight in relation to the cabinets and the countertop. To raise or lower one or both sides, use an adjustable wrench to turn the feet at the bottom of the unit. Wiggle the dishwasher to test that it rests solidly on all four feet.

Once satisfied with the dishwasher's position, open the door and find the mounting tabs (usually on the top edge, sometimes on the sides). Drill pilot holes. To avoid drilling up through the countertop, wrap a piece of tape on the drill bit to mark the depth to stop. Drive short screws into the holes to anchor the dishwasher to the countertop.

TOILETS

Considering how often they are used—typically, thousands of times per year—most toilets are remarkably durable. The basic toilet is made of porcelain or vitreous china and lasts practically forever, as long as it doesn't get cracked at some point. The mechanical inner workings, however, are somewhat complicated, so it is not surprising that they occasionally need repair. Fortunately no repair is too tough for a determined do-it-yourselfer.

Sanitary conditions

Many people are understandably reluctant to touch the water in a toilet. With a few precautions, however, contact with unsanitary water can be avoided.

Water from the toilet bowl cannot back up into the tank; water in the tank is just as clean as water from a faucet. If you clean the bowl and flush several times, even the water in the bowl will be clean.

When a toilet is clogged, sewage may back up and overflow onto the floor. Wear heavy-duty rubber gloves when cleaning.

You may need to insert a plunger into sewage to clear a clog. After doing so, clean the plunger thoroughly—inside and out—with hot water and detergent.

How it works

A toilet bowl has a built-in trap. When water rushes in from the tank through a series of openings under the bowl rim, the water in the bowl is pushed through the trap and into the sewer line. Some bowls have a jet opening located near the bottom for increased flushing power.

A wax ring seals the bowl to the toilet flange on the floor. Flushed water flows through a closet bend below the floor, and out to a large drain stack. This arrangement ensures that anything that makes it through the toilet will reach the stack and exit the house.

There are two mechanisms in the tank. The flush valve has a rubber flapper attached to a chain or, in older toilets, a rubber stopper attached to a lift rod. When the flapper or stopper rests on the flush valve seat, water is sealed inside the tank. When you push down on the flush handle, the flapper or stopper is raised, providing an opening for water to run out of the tank and into the bowl. When the tank is nearly empty, the flapper or stopper settles down onto the seat again, sealing the tank for filling.

The other tank mechanism is the fill valve assembly, which squirts water into the tank until the water reaches a certain level, then automatically shuts off. Most older toilets have a brass ballcock fill valve attached to a float ball; when the ball floats high enough, the water automatically shuts off. A diaphragm fill valve is also attached to a float ball. A float-cup fill valve replaces the float ball with a plastic cup that slides up and down its shaft as the water rises and falls.

If the fill valve fails to shut off, the excess water will flow down the overflow tube and into the bowl.

An emergency fix

If water starts welling up when you flush the toilet rather than swirling down into the bowl, you may be able to keep water from spilling onto the floor if you act quickly. Remove the tank lid, reach into the tank (remember, this water is clean), and push down on the flapper or stopper until it settles on the flush valve seat. Water will stop flowing. Take steps to clear the clog (page 89) before flushing the toilet again.

Nearly all toilet problems can be fixed quickly and inexpensively.

CHAPTER PREVIEW

Troubleshooting and repairs
page 88

Clearing a clog
page 89

Eliminating run-on
page 90

Installing a new float cup
page 91

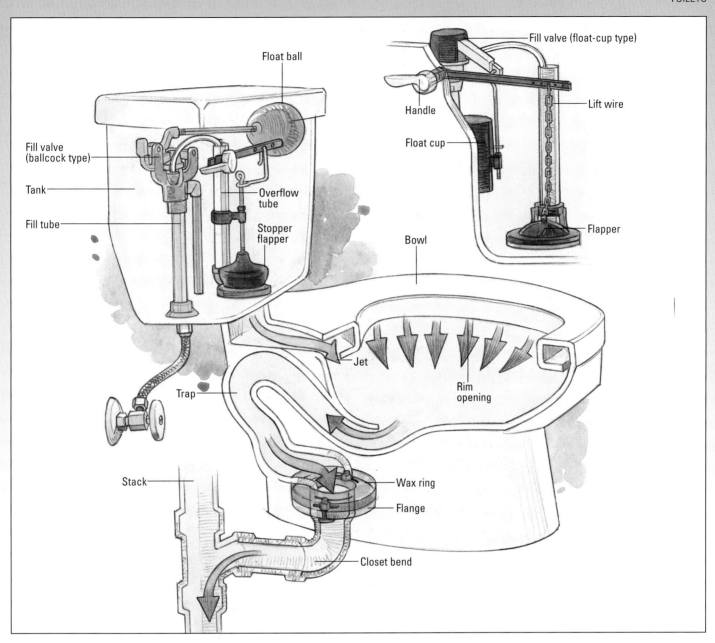

Float ball

Fill valve (float-cup type)

Fill valve
(ballcock type)

Handle

Lift wire

Tank

Float cup

Overflow
tube

Fill tube

Stopper
flapper

Flapper

Bowl

Jet

Rim
opening

Trap

Stack

Wax ring

Flange

Closet bend

**Seeping and
phantom flushes**
page 92

**Leaks from
the tank**
page 93

Replacing a toilet
page 94

*No matter how old it is, all the moving parts
in a toilet—the fill valve, the stopper, and the
float—can be replaced, either with exact
duplicate parts or with new mechanisms that
perform the same duties reliably. If it's a leak,
it can be fixed either by tightening a bolt or
by replacing a gasket. In the most extreme
instance, you will have to pull up the toilet and
replace the wax ring. A clog can almost always
be cleared with a plunger or auger. The only
time you need to replace a toilet is if the tank
or the bowl is cracked.*

TROUBLESHOOTING AND REPAIRS

No matter how old or complicated a toilet may appear, replacement parts are readily available and usually are not difficult to install. In fact, the only reason to replace a toilet is if it is cracked— or simply out of style.

It's important to make the correct diagnosis before starting a repair. A look under the tank lid quickly reveals the cause of many problems. If flushes are incomplete, check that the water level reaches the proper height—an inch or less from the top of the overflow tube. If the toilet constantly hisses, or if water seeps into the bowl, the tank water level may be too high. The excess water is slowly overflowing into the overflow tube and into the bowl. Adjusting the water level is usually a simple matter. In some cases, however, the fill valve may need to be repaired or replaced.

If the toilet is clogged, use a plunger or an auger to clear the problem.

If water seeps out the bottom of the bowl when the toilet is flushed, the wax ring needs to be replaced (page 94–95).

Solutions to common toilet problems

Bowl overflows or will not flush freely: Clear a clog with a plunger, pressure plunger, or toilet auger (page 89).

Toilet does not flush: Check that the handle is connected to the flapper via a chain or to the stopper via a lift rod (page 92). Check that water is turned on and running into the tank.

Incomplete (short) flushes: Check the water level in tank and adjust the float ball, chain, or lift rod (page 90). Flush the toilet and watch the flapper or the stopper; if it goes down too soon, replace it (page 92).

Handle is loose or tight: Tighten the nut holding the handle to the tank. Check the handle's connection to the wire or the lift rod (page 90).

Water sprays out of the tank: Reattach the fill tube to the overflow tube (page 91).

Run-on: Adjust the float ball, stopper, or cup. Replace a leaky float ball or stopper (page 90). If these measures do not bring the water level below the top of the overflow tube, repair or replace the fill valve (page 91).

Water seeps continuously into the bowl, making it necessary to jiggle the handle; occasional "phantom flushes": Clean the flush valve seat and adjust the flapper or stopper. You may need to replace the flapper or stopper (page 92).

Leak from the tank: Check and tighten water supply connection. Tighten tank bolts. If the tank is cracked, replace it (page 94).

Leak from the base of the bowl: Remove the toilet, replace the wax ring, and reinstall the toilet. If the bowl is cracked, replace it (pages 94–95).

PRESTART CHECKLIST

☐ **TIME**
Less than an hour for most repairs

☐ **TOOLS**
Screwdriver, groove-joint pliers, adjustable wrench, toilet plunger, toilet auger, locking pliers, small mirror, bottle brush

☐ **SKILLS**
Making simple plumbing corrections

☐ **PREP**
Place a drop cloth on the floor and set the tank lid where it won't get damaged.

☐ **MATERIALS**
Repair parts, perhaps a new float-cup assembly

THREE TYPES OF FILL VALVES

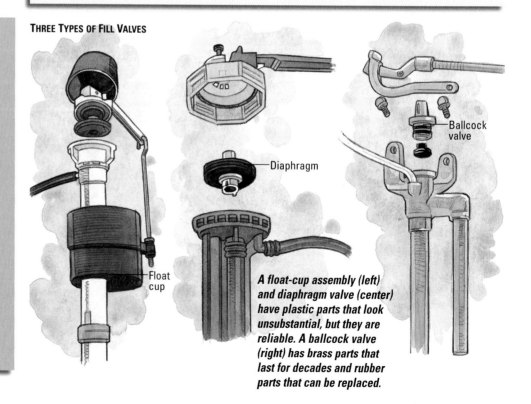

Diaphragm

Ballcock valve

Float cup

A float-cup assembly (left) and diaphragm valve (center) have plastic parts that look unsubstantial, but they are reliable. A ballcock valve (right) has brass parts that last for decades and rubber parts that can be replaced.

Clearing a clog

Plunger

1 You can usually clear a clog with a toilet plunger. Insert the plunger flange into the hole at the bottom of the bowl until it seals. Push and pull vigorously several times. Repeat the process as many as 10 times.

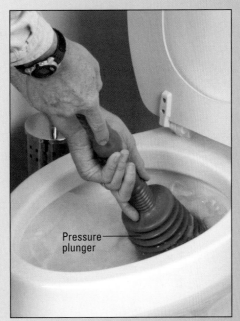

Pressure plunger

2 For tenacious clogs, this type of plunger exerts even greater pressure. Seat it firmly in the bowl hole, and pump it until you feel the pressure build. When the clog clears, you will feel a sudden loss of pressure.

Toilet auger

3 If plunging does not clear a clog, use a toilet auger. Pull the auger's handle up, insert the auger, then crank while pushing down. The auger may push an obstruction through, or it may grab the obstruction so you can then pull it out (see *page 27*).

Water-saving toilets

U.S. codes require that new toilets use no more than 1.6 gallons of water per flush; older toilets use from 3 to 5 gallons. Many early 1.6-gallon models, made in the mid-1990s, do not flush well because the manufacturers simply reduced the tank size without changing the design. If yours is one of these, you may want to replace it with a newer model that flushes more completely.

Newer gravity-flush models increase pressure by virtue of different hole designs that maximize water flow.

For even more flushing power, consider spending more for a pressure-assisted toilet, which uses pressurized air to make the water flow faster. However, this design is noisy.

A pump-assisted toilet creates great pressure with less noise, but it is expensive, and has an electric pump that must be hooked up to power.

WHAT IF...
The clog is severe?

Auger

Occasionally a clog is too stubborn to be cleared by a plunger or auger. (Dumping construction materials, such as joint compound or tile-setting mortar, into a toilet can lead to this condition.) If you run into this problem, turn off the water, drain the tank, and remove the toilet (*page 94*). Turn the toilet upside down and chip away any caked-on debris. Then run an auger through it backward.

Eliminating run-on

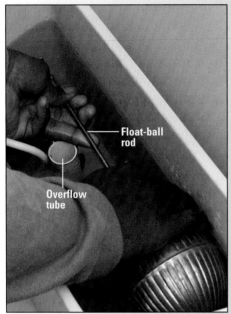

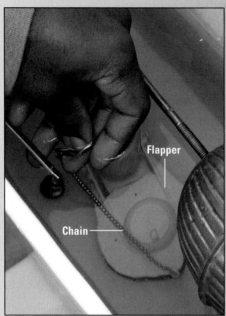

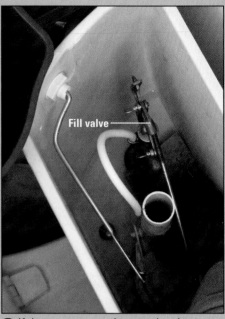

1 If water runs continuously, remove the tank lid and check the water level. If water is running over the top of the overflow tube, lower the level. If there is a float ball, bend its rod so the ball sits lower.

2 A kinked or tangled chain may cause run-on. Detach it from the handle arm, undo the kink or tangle, and reattach it so there is about ½ inch of slack in the chain when the flapper is seated.

3 If these measures do not solve the problem, the fill valve needs to be repaired or replaced. The tank must be emptied for this and other repairs. **Shut off water to the toilet** and flush the toilet to remove most of the water. Use a sponge to remove the rest of the water.

WHAT IF...
The float cup needs adjusting?

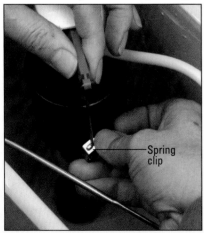

To adjust water level when there is a float-cup assembly, pinch the spring clip and slide the float cup up or down—up to raise the water level, down to lower it.

Adjusting the lift wire

The lift wire attached to a stopper must slide smoothly. If it doesn't, straighten it. You may need to bend the wire that connects the lift wire to the handle. Work carefully and test thoroughly until the lift wire slides without interruption every time.

Making handle adjustments

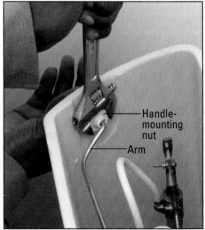

If a handle jiggles loosely, tighten the nut that connects it to the tank. Check the arm that connects to the flapper or stopper as well. Make sure it does not bump into any mechanisms in the tank.

Installing a new float cup

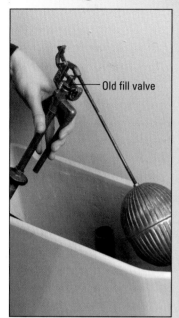

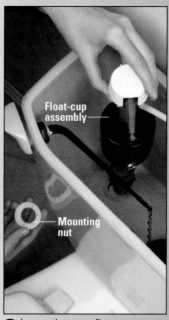

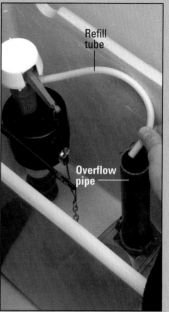

1 **Shut off water at the stop valve.** Disconnect the supply tube. Clamp locking pliers onto the nut at the base of the old assembly. Under the tank, use an adjustable wrench to remove the nut. Lift the assembly out.

2 Insert the new float-cup assembly through the hole in the tank. Hold it in place with locking pliers and tighten the mounting nut under the tank. Make sure the cup will be clear of any obstructions.

3 Remove the flapper or stopper. Slide the new flapper down the overflow pipe and adjust it so it flops down onto the center of the flush-valve seat. Attach the chain to it so there is about ½ inch of slack.

4 Clip the refill tube to the overflow tube. Reattach the supply tube and turn the shutoff valve back on. Let the tank fill and check for leaks.

Repairing a ballcock valve

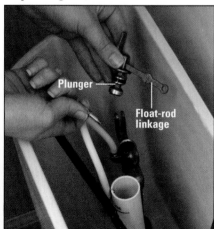

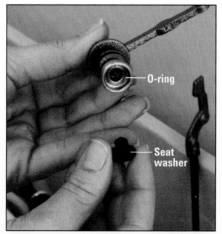

1 If only the rubber parts of a ballcock valve are damaged, you can replace them. Remove the float-rod linkage, which is attached with two screws. Use pliers to pull out the plunger.

2 Clean away sediment in the valve, using a toothbrush or a soft wire brush. If the O-rings and the seat washer are worn, you may find it difficult to find replacements. In that case, buy a new float-cup assembly and replace the entire assembly (above).

WHAT IF...
There is a diaphragm valve?

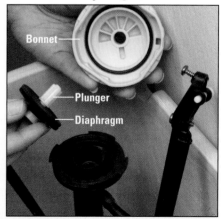

Remove the clip or screws from the top of a diaphragm fill valve and lift out the bonnet. Pull out the plunger. Clean away any debris or slime. If the plunger or the diaphragm is worn, replace it or replace the entire unit.

Seeping and phantom flushes

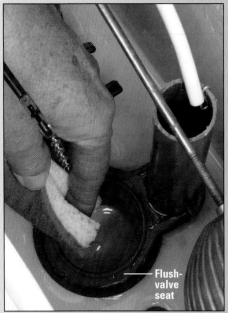

Water runs into bowl: If water sometimes gurgles into the bowl until you jiggle the handle, the handle may be loose or in need of adjustment. Metal handle arms can be adjusted by gentle bending. The lift rod or chain may be snagged or stuck—adjust them or replace if needed.

Phantom flushes: If water slowly seeps into the bowl, you may or may not hear it. A faint, "phantom" flush may occur every so often. In this case, the flapper or stopper is not sealing tightly against the flush-valve seat. **Shut off the water** and flush; then clean the seat with a nonmetallic scrubbing pad.

Persistent problems: See whether the flapper or stopper is centered in the seat. Raising or twisting a flapper may solve the problem. If not, install a new one. Bring the old flapper to a home center so you can buy an exact replacement. If the new flapper does not seat tightly, try a different type.

WHAT IF...
The toilet has a weak flush?

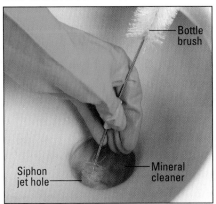

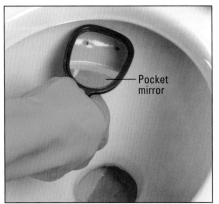

1 If water flows weakly into the bowl, partially blocked rim openings or a blocked jet may be the culprit. **Shut off the water** and flush; then pour mineral cleaner into the bowl. Clean a siphon jet with a bottle brush.

2 Brush the rim openings with the cleaner and allow several minutes for it to soak in; repeat several times. A mirror will help you see if any openings are clogged. Auger a rim opening with a piece of insulated wire or a very small bottle brush.

A replacement flapper kit

Replacement flappers are available for virtually every toilet. This kit is ideal if you're having trouble getting a flapper to seal. It comes with its own seat, which seals tightly on top of an existing seat.

Leaks from the tank

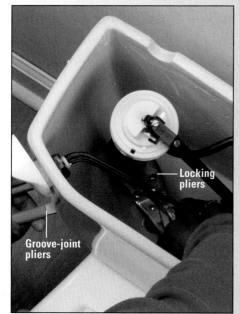

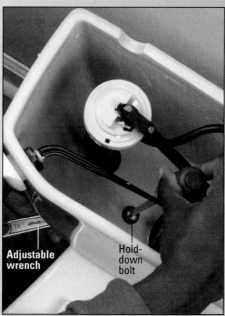

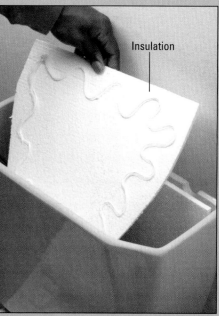

Leak at supply: If water leaks where the supply tube enters the tank, **shut off the water** and flush. Gently clamp locking pliers to the nut inside the tank and tighten the mounting nut under the toilet. If this doesn't solve the problem, you may need to replace the mounting-nut gasket inside the tank.

Leak between tank and bowl: Shut off the water and flush. With an adjustable wrench holding the nut under the tank, tighten the screw inside the tank. Don't overtighten; you may crack the tank. If this doesn't solve the problem, replace the rubber washers under the hold-down bolts.

Sweaty tank: If drops of condensation appear on the tank, buy a tank insulating kit. Drain and dry the tank. Cut each insulation piece to fit and attach it with the adhesive provided.

Replacing a toilet seat

To remove an existing toilet seat, pry up any caps at the back of the seat to reveal the screw heads. Clamp locking pliers to the nut below and unscrew. Some plastic nuts have wings, so you do not need the pliers.

If old metal bolts are rusted tight, spray them with penetrating oil. If necessary, cut through the bolts with a hacksaw.

Clean the top of the bowl. Hold the new seat centered over the bowl as you tighten the nuts.

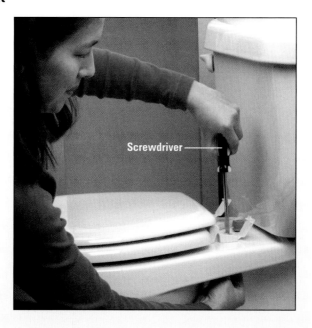

STANLEY PRO TIP

Water from the bowl means the toilet needs resetting

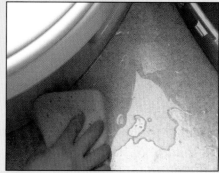

If water leaks from the bottom of the bowl when you flush, check the bowl for cracks. If there are none, the wax ring needs to be replaced. Follow the steps on *pages 94–95* to remove the toilet, install a new wax ring, and reinstall.

REPLACING A TOILET

Most new toilets come in two boxes, one for the bowl and one for the tank with all the moving parts installed. Attaching the tank to the bowl should take only half an hour or so.

The steps at right show how to assemble the tank and bowl, then how to install the toilet. You may choose to install the bowl first and then attach the tank. If the existing toilet is heavy, you may want to detach the tank from the bowl before removing it. Keep your back straight and lift with the legs. Arrange for a helper if possible. Follow these same steps if your toilet is leaking from the base and you need to replace the wax ring.

Choosing a toilet

You may choose a pressure- or pump-assisted toilet. Most toilets have mounting holes 12 inches from the back wall, but some are 10 inches away. Measure the old toilet carefully and buy one with the same dimensions.

PRESTART CHECKLIST

☐ **TIME**
About 2 hours to remove an existing toilet and install a new one

☐ **TOOLS**
Adjustable wrench, screwdriver, putty knife, hacksaw, utility knife

☐ **SKILLS**
Making simple plumbing connections, assembling a toilet

☐ **PREP**
Shut off water to the toilet, flush; use a sponge or rag to remove all the water you can from the tank and the bowl.

☐ **MATERIALS**
Toilet, flanged wax ring, perhaps a nonflanged ring, flange bolts, plumber's putty

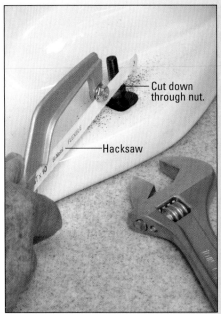

Cut down through nut.

Hacksaw

1 **Shut off water at the stop valve.** Disconnect the supply tube at the tank and wall. Pry off any decorative caps and unscrew the nuts holding the bowl to the floor. If the nuts are frozen, cut through them with a hacksaw.

Old putty

2 If there is a bead of caulk around the bowl at the floor, cut through it with a utility knife. If the toilet is old, check to see if the tank is bolted to the wall and remove the bolts. Grasp the toilet bowl on each side, pick it up, and set it on a drop cloth.

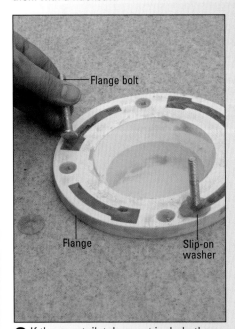

Flange bolt

Flange

Slip-on washer

6 If the new toilet does not include them, buy new flange bolts. Use slip-on plastic washers to hold them temporarily in place, pointing straight up. Remove the rag from the hole.

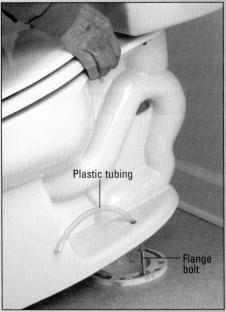

Plastic tubing

Flange bolt

7 Lower the toilet bowl so that the flange bolts poke through the holes. If it is difficult to line up the holes with the bolts, place a piece of plastic tubing over the bolt to guide it through the base as you lower the bowl.

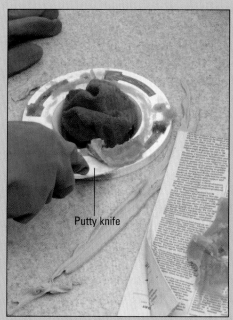

3 Place a large, damp rag in the hole to seal off sewer gas. Scrape away all putty and wax from the floor. Finish cleaning with a rag. If you are reinstalling the existing toilet, clean the bottom of its bowl in the same way.

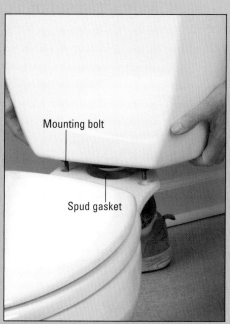

Mounting bolt

Spud gasket

4 Assemble the tank and the bowl of a new toilet, following the manufacturer's instructions. A large spud gasket seals the opening below the flush-valve seat. Place a rubber washer under the head of each mounting bolt. Do not overtighten the nuts.

Wax ring

Flange

5 Press a new wax ring, flange pointed out (or down), on the underside of the toilet bowl. (Not all toilets or drainpipes accept a flanged ring; wax rings without the flange are also available.)

8 Press down on the bowl with both hands to seat the toilet firmly on the wax ring. Check the position of the toilet by looking at the toilet tank: it should be parallel to the wall and level.

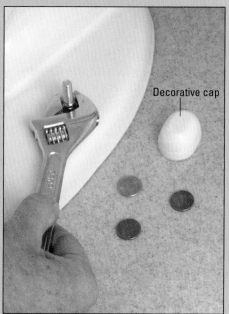

Decorative cap

9 Tighten the nut on each side of the bowl, alternating sides. If the floor is uneven, use pennies as shims. Avoid overtightening. Stop tightening when the bowl feels solid when you sit on it. Carefully cut off the tip of each bolt and cover with a decorative cap.

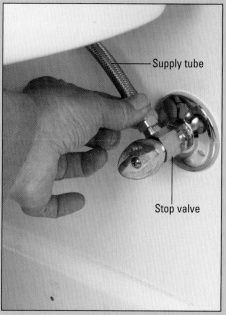

Supply tube

Stop valve

10 Connect the supply tube, turn on the water, and test.

PIPE REPAIRS

If a pipe suddenly springs a leak, you may be able to make a temporary repair by wrapping it tightly with electrician's tape. But a more permanent repair must be made as soon as possible.

If a pipe clamp *(page 97)* does not solve the problem, you'll need to remove and replace sections of pipe, and possibly fittings as well. This chapter shows how to cut, assemble, and join copper, steel, and plastic pipe, as well as how to make repairs to cast-iron pipe. In addition, it shows how to repair and replace valves, quiet noisy pipes, and thaw frozen pipes.

Pipe repair can be time-consuming, especially if the pipes are hard to reach. You may spend more time cutting into and patching walls than working on the plumbing.

Running new lines

You can use the techniques in this chapter to make a pipe repair, or to add a new line for additional service. Usually, simply installing a tee-fitting allows you to run a new supply line. Armed with this knowledge, you can tackle a simple project like a laundry room *(pages 76–77)* as long as the drain line does not have to travel more than about 5 feet.

To install new service, on the other hand, is usually a complicated matter. Drain lines in particular must follow strict guidelines and must be properly vented *(pages 10–11)*. Contact a professional plumber for any project more complicated than a simple laundry room hookup.

STANLEY PRO TIP

Buy plenty of parts

Many people find the bulk of time spent on a home plumbing repair is actually used for shopping rather than doing the plumbing. Minimize trips with careful planning. List and buy everything that you may possibly need. Don't be afraid of buying too much; you can always return items you don't use.

Pipe repairs call for learning special skills. With a little practice, you can handle most jobs.

CHAPTER PREVIEW

Repairs to copper pipe
page 98

Repairs to plastic pipe
page 102

Repairs to steel pipe
page 104

Gas pipe and connectors
page 106

Repairs to cast-iron pipe
page 107

If a galvanized or copper supply pipe gets punctured, a pipe clamp makes a permanent repair, as long as the pipe is exposed. If the pipe is hidden inside a wall, codes require that the pipe be replaced. To install a clamp, shut off water to the pipe and sand smooth the area around the damage. Center the rubber gasket over the puncture and tighten the nuts on the clamp.

Adjustable wrench

Galvanized-steel pipe

Pipe clamp

While a properly applied clamp makes a permanent repair, you may prefer to splice in a replacement with like material. To make repairs to copper pipe, see pages 98–101; plastic, pages 102–103; steel, pages 104–105; cast-iron, page 107.

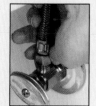

Leaks at stop valves and supply tubes
page 108

Installing a stop valve on copper pipe
page 110

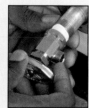

Installing a stop valve on steel pipe
page 111

Repairing shutoff valves
page 112

Silencing pipe noises
page 113

Thawing pipes and winterizing
page 114

REPAIRS TO COPPER PIPE

Because of its durability, copper is the preferred material for most water supply lines. Even if you have galvanized or plastic supply pipe in your house, you may want to use a transition fitting *(pages 104–105)* and switch to copper when making a repair or extending a line.

The process of soldering the parts together, called "sweating," may appear daunting, but with an hour or two of practice you are almost certain to get the hang of it. For practice, on a worktable with a vise, sweat 10 or more fittings onto pipes until you feel confident you're able to produce joints that are secure.

Type M copper pipe is fine for most residential work. Buy lead-free solder and flux paste.

Compression fittings require no special skills to install, but they are expensive. Use them only where they will be exposed; any joints hidden in a wall must be sweated.

Sweating a large copper drain line calls for a large propane torch; you're probably better off hiring a pro for such work.

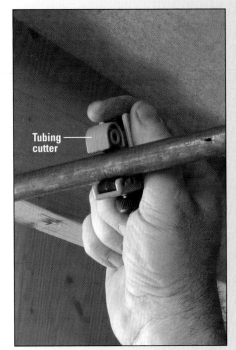

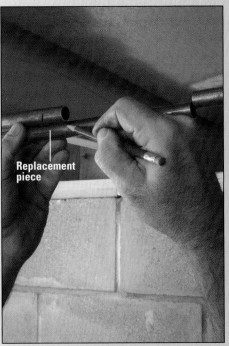

1 **Shut off the water.** Use a tubing cutter to cut each side of the damaged area. Screw the cutter tight, rotate it a full turn, tighten, and rotate again until the cut is complete. If there is not enough room, cut with a hacksaw. Exert gentle pressure to avoid flattening the pipe and file off burrs.

2 If either of the existing pipes is moveable, you can use standard couplings *(page 14)*. If not, use slip couplings (Step 4). Measure the replacement piece by holding it in place. It should be the same length. Cut the new piece with a tubing cutter.

PRESTART CHECKLIST

☐ **TIME**
An hour or two to make most repairs

☐ **TOOLS**
Groove-joint pliers, tubing cutter, hacksaw, propane torch, flux brush, sandpaper, wire reaming brush

☐ **SKILLS**
Using a pipe cutter, handling a propane torch

☐ **PREP**
Shut off the water and drain the line. Position a piece of sheet metal to protect any flammable surfaces.

☐ **MATERIALS**
Copper pipe and fittings, flux, solder

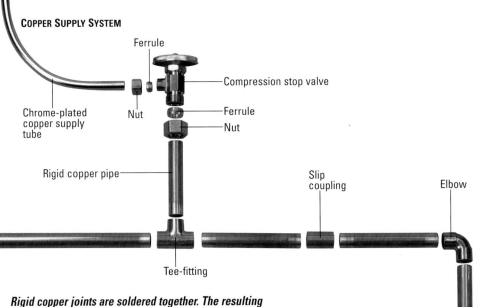

COPPER SUPPLY SYSTEM

Rigid copper joints are soldered together. The resulting joints, if made correctly, are actually stronger than the pipe itself. To add a new supply line, install a tee-fitting. Use a compression fitting only if it will remain exposed.

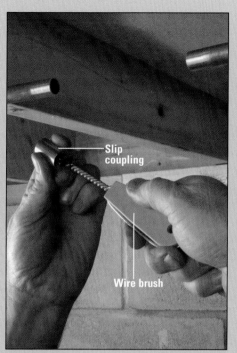

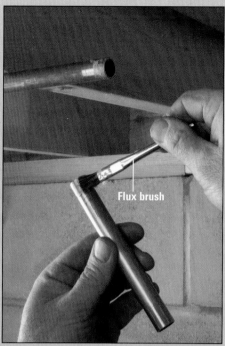

3 Sand the outside of all the pipe ends with emery cloth or sandpaper or use a combination wire brush. The sanded area should be clean and shiny, revealing untarnished copper.

4 Slip couplings can be pushed all the way onto a pipe; they do not have the middle ridge that standard couplings have. Use a wire brush to ream out the insides of the fittings. These should be shiny as well. Sanding and reaming are essential to making a secure joint.

5 Using the little brush that comes with the flux, brush a medium-thick layer of flux all the way around each pipe end that will be joined. Flux helps solder adhere to the pipe surface.

Combination wire brush

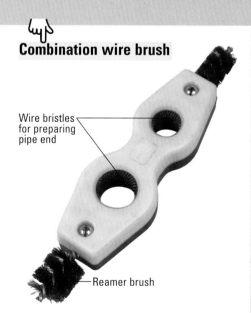

This handy tool reams out the insides of fittings and takes the place of emery cloth or sandpaper for preparing the outside of each pipe end.

STANLEY PRO TIP

Bread trick for wet pipe

If a pipe keeps dripping after you have shut off the water, jam a wad of soft white bread (it should have no whole grain or crust in it) into the pipe. Sweat the joint quickly, before the bread gets wet. Once the repair is made and the water turned on, open a nearby faucet. The bread will dissolve and flush out.

WHAT IF...
You need to bend copper pipe?

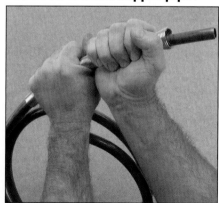

If a repair calls for a gentle bend, use a tubing bender. This springlike tool comes in several sizes. Slip it over flexible copper pipe, slide it over the point where the bend is needed, and carefully make the bend. The bender keeps the pipe from kinking.

Repairs to copper pipe (continued)

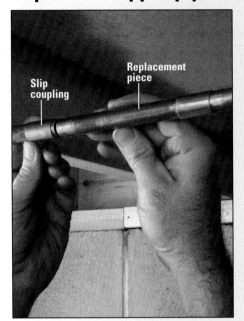

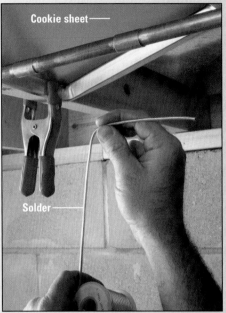

6 A slip coupling slides all the way onto a pipe. Slide a coupling on each side, position the replacement piece, and slide the couplings back halfway. (To install a standard coupling or elbow, give it a slight twist as you push it all the way into place.)

7 **Protect any nearby surfaces from the torch flame** by clamping in place an old cookie sheet or a piece of sheet metal. **Keep a home fire extinguisher handy in case wood starts to smolder.** Pull about 10 inches of solder away from the spool and bend about 3 inches at a convenient angle.

8 If your propane torch has an automatic igniter *(page 9),* turn on the gas and squeeze the trigger. If not, turn the gas on low, light the end with a match or striker, and open the valve until you have an interior blue flame that is 2 to 3 inches long (see flame in Step 9).

Patch a pipe with a tape kit

While not as fail-safe as a sweated patch, fiberglass patch tape can provide a quick, long-lasting cure for a leaky pipe. The kit includes tape impregnated with resin, gloves, and a lubricant that helps you squeeze out voids and bubbles.

STANLEY PRO TIP

Remove stem before soldering

A shutoff valve may have rubber washers and O-rings, or other parts that can be damaged by heat. Before sweating a valve, remove all the inner parts.

It will take more time to heat up a brass valve than it takes to heat a copper fitting, so have patience. Apply solder as you would for a fitting (above).

Allow the fitting to cool before replacing the inner parts.

Compression fittings

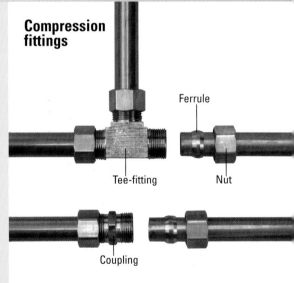

Compression fittings often make sense in tight places where it is difficult to solder. To install one, slide the nut, then the ferrule, onto the pipe. Slip the fitting onto the pipe, slide the ferrule into the fitting, and tighten the nut. No thread tape or pipe compound is necessary.

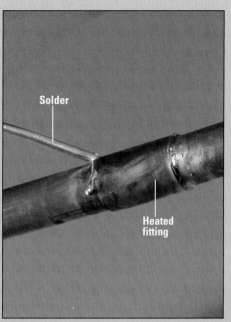

9 Aim the torch so the tip of the blue flame touches the middle of the fitting. When the flux starts to sizzle (usually after five seconds or so), move the flame to the opposite side and heat it briefly.

10 Touch the tip of the solder to the joint. If the solder melts immediately and sucks into the joint, move the solder around so the entire joint is soldered. If it does not melt, heat the fitting for a few more seconds and try again. Never heat the pipe or the solder directly.

11 Once solder has been sucked into the joint all around, wipe the joint with a rag to smooth the solder and eliminate any drips. **Fold the rag several times and/or wear leather gloves. Repeat for the other side of the fitting. Check the work area an hour later to be sure nothing is smoldering.**

WHAT IF...
A fitting leaks?

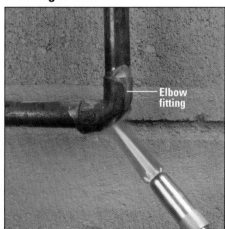

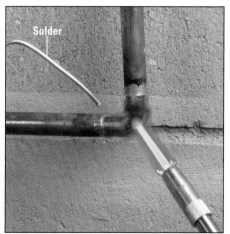

1 If water leaks from a fitting, replace it. Aim a propane torch at the fitting so the tip of the blue flame just touches the center of the fitting. When it starts to sizzle, heat the opposite side.

2 Immediately pull the fitting away from the pipes, using two pliers. If it fails to come apart, reheat and try again. Sand the pipe ends thoroughly to remove any trace of old solder.

3 Ream the inside of a new fitting, apply flux to the pipe ends, and sweat the joints, as shown in Steps 7 to 11 above.

REPAIRS TO PLASTIC PIPE

White PVC pipe is the current material of choice for most drain lines. Existing black ABS pipe can be replaced with PVC. If you use a transition fitting, you can connect PVC to galvanized drainpipe. Special fittings also allow you to attach PVC to cast-iron pipe.

Using PVC for supply lines is not allowed by many building codes; check with your local building inspector before using it. CPVC is approved for many outdoor uses, such as lawn sprinkler systems.

Plastic pipe is easy to assemble, but take care to do it right. Joints must be primed and glued completely or they may leak. If you install a fitting that makes a turn, such as a tee or an elbow, use alignment marks to ensure the fitting faces the right way. There is no correcting mistakes—if a glued joint points in the wrong direction, you must cut out the error and start over. PVC pipe is inexpensive, so before you tackle the real thing, practice cutting and gluing pieces until you feel proficient.

1 Cut PVC pipe using a PVC saw, a hacksaw, or most any saw with fine teeth. A miter box helps hold the pipe to make perpendicular cuts.

PVC saw

2 Scrape the inside and outside of the sawed edge with a utility knife to remove burrs.

PRESTART CHECKLIST

☐ **TIME**
About an hour to make a simple repair

☐ **TOOLS**
PVC saw and miter box, utility knife, tape measure, felt-tipped pen

☐ **SKILLS**
Measuring, cutting PVC

☐ **PREP**
Spread a drop cloth to catch any spilled primer and glue.

☐ **MATERIALS**
PVC pipe and fittings, primer, cement

SAFETY FIRST
Beware of fumes

PVC primer and cement are flammable and give off unpleasant and dangerous fumes. Keep flames and sparks away and open a window to provide ventilation. Cap the cans when they are not in use. Tighten the caps firmly when done.

Also be sure to use the correct primer and cement for your type of plastic pipe. PVC and CPVC use different products. The wrong primer and cement can ruin the installation.

WHAT IF...
Flexible plastic is used for a repair?

Compression/threaded coupling

Compression coupling

Flexible PEX supply pipe is approved in some areas. The pipe's flexibility makes it easy to turn corners. Fittings attach with compression joints, so no gluing is needed and mistakes can be easily corrected. However these fittings cannot be hidden behind a wall surface.

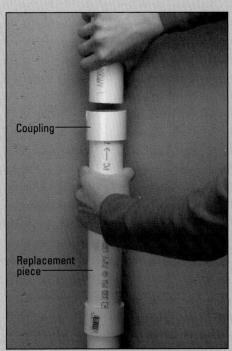

Coupling

Replacement piece

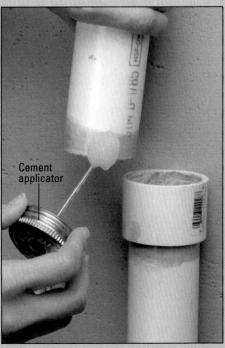

Cement applicator

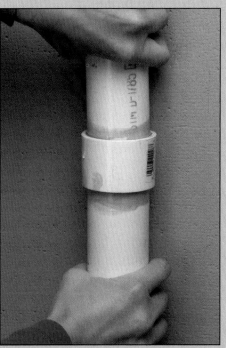

3 Assemble the pieces in a dry run to make sure everything fits. Disassemble the pieces, keeping track of the order in which they will be reassembled.

4 Apply primer to the pipe ends and to the insides of the fittings. The strip of primer on the pipe should be wide enough so that some can still be seen after the fitting is attached. Apply cement to the outside of the pipe, then to the inside of the coupling.

5 Immediately insert the pipe into the fitting and give it a slight twist. Some cement should ooze around the joint. Hold the joint for about 20 seconds, then wipe away any excess cement. Wait at least 30 minutes before running drain water through the pipes.

STANLEY PRO TIP: **Repair to a supply pipe**

Cut PVC or CPVC supply pipe with the scissors-like PVC pipe cutter. Deburr, make a dry run, apply primer, and glue pieces together just as you would for drainpipe (Steps 2 to 5 above).

Because water pressure is greater in a supply pipe than a drainpipe, wait several hours for the cement to fully cure before you run water through the pipes.

A similar tool can be used to neatly cut flexible pipe and tubing.

PVC pipe cutter

Adding a tee-fitting for a new line

To add a new drain line, cut the pipe and install a tee-fitting. Use alignment marks to make sure the tee is facing the right way. Once the tee is installed, assemble the lengths of pipe and fittings needed to reach the new location.

REPAIRS TO STEEL PIPE

Galvanized steel pipe is strong, but it corrodes. If you are adding a new line, make the transition to copper pipe. However, if only a replacement piece or two is needed, it makes sense to stick with galvanized.

Because pipe threads go only one way, you cannot simply remove a piece in the middle of a run and replace it. Instead, cut the pipe, remove both halves, and install a union—a special fitting that allows you to install pipes on each side.

It is not practical for a homeowner to cut and thread steel pipe. Disassemble the pipes and carefully measure to determine the lengths of pipe needed. A plumbing supply store or home center can cut pieces to fit. Or purchase pipes that are roughly the size you need, plus nipples (short lengths of pipe threaded at each end) of various sizes and several couplings. That way you should be equipped with all the pieces needed to finish a run.

PRESTART CHECKLIST

☐ **TIME**
A couple of hours for most repairs

☐ **TOOLS**
Two pipe wrenches, groove-joint pliers, hacksaw or reciprocating saw with metal-cutting blade, tape measure, felt-tipped pen

☐ **SKILLS**
Measuring and assembling threaded pipe

☐ **PREP**
Shut off water and drain the line.

☐ **MATERIALS**
Lengths of galvanized pipe, fittings (especially a union), pipe-thread tape, nipples

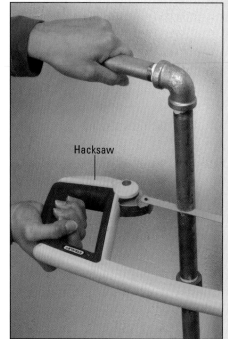

1 **Shut off water.** Cut through the pipe that needs to be replaced, using a hacksaw or a reciprocating saw equipped with a metal-cutting blade.

Pipe wrench

2 To remove each piece, stabilize the fitting with one pipe wrench and twist the pipe counterclockwise with another pipe wrench. Select nipples and a union that will add up to the proper length for the repair.

GALVANIZED PIPE SYSTEM

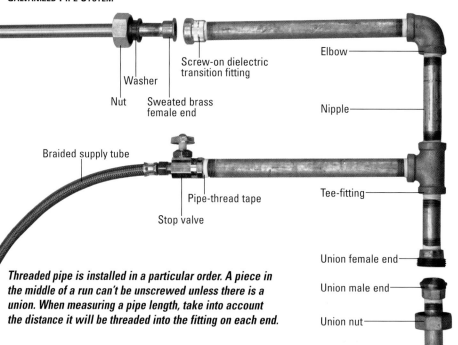

Nut
Washer
Sweated brass female end
Screw-on dielectric transition fitting
Braided supply tube
Stop valve
Pipe-thread tape
Elbow
Nipple
Tee-fitting
Union female end
Union male end
Union nut

Threaded pipe is installed in a particular order. A piece in the middle of a run can't be unscrewed unless there is a union. When measuring a pipe length, take into account the distance it will be threaded into the fitting on each end.

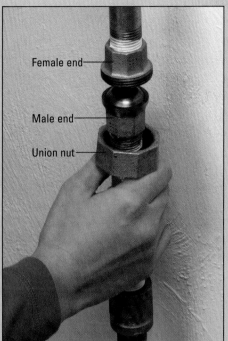

3 Before screwing a pipe into a fitting, wrap pipe-thread tape around it clockwise, as shown, several times. Finish by snapping the tape and smoothing the end over the threads. Screw in the pipe by hand, then keep turning with a pipe wrench to get it very tight.

4 Install the female threaded part of the union on one of the pieces. On the other piece, slip on the union nut, then tighten the unthreaded male part.

5 Seat the male part into the female part, check that the two pipes form a straight line, and slide the nut onto the male part. It should screw on easily; if not, the pipes may need to be realigned. Tighten the nut with a pipe wrench.

Steel pipe touching copper pipe will corrode and leak

Dielectric union

The combination of copper, steel, and water creates a small electric current that corrodes copper, causing the joint to fail and clogging the inside of the pipes. To avoid this situation, use a dielectric (nonconductive) union. It is lined with a nonmetallic sleeve that prevents copper from touching steel. To install a dielectric union, screw the threaded part onto the steel pipe. Before sweating the brass fitting of the copper pipe, slip on the nut and sleeve and push them well away from the heat of the torch. Once the fitting is sweated and cools, join the two parts. Tighten the nut with groove-joint pliers.

WHAT IF...
The water pressure is low?

If water pressure is low in your house, partially clogged galvanized supply pipes may be the cause. The rough coating of zinc on galvanized pipes causes mineral deposits to form over time. Most of the sediment collects in horizontal pipes. If you replace the horizontal pipes where the water line enters the house, you stand a good chance of increasing water flow to the entire house.

If a certain faucet has low pressure, you may be able to locate and replace a section of horizontal pipe directly below it to increase flow to that faucet.

STANLEY PRO TIP

Joining steel pipe

When joining steel pipe, pipe-thread tape and pipe-joint compound accomplish the same goals: They lubricate the threads to make it easier to tighten the connection, and they fill tiny spaces between the threads. Thread tape is less messy, but pipe-joint compound is easier to apply if the pipe is against a wall. Follow these tips for tightening the joint:
■ In a tight spot, tighten the joint as far as you can using a pair of groove-joint pliers, then switch to a pipe wrench.
■ Always finish tightening by using a pipe wrench at least 14 inches long; a smaller tool won't have enough leverage.
■ If a fitting is so tight it won't budge with a pipe wrench, slip a length of 1¼-inch steel pipe over the handle to increase the leverage and add to the persuasiveness of the wrench.

GAS PIPE AND CONNECTORS

Plumbing codes require that black threaded pipe be used for gas lines. Assembly techniques are the same as for galvanized water pipe *(pages 104–105)*.

Usually black pipe is not used for water supply. The one exception: It is often used for the supply pipes that bring water to a heating system's boiler, an installation for professionals only.

If a gas smell is strong, take emergency steps (see below). If you suspect a slow gas leak, carefully work to find the source. Open windows and doors to ventilate the room. Take steps to ensure there will be no sparks or flames in the room while you work.

PRESTART CHECKLIST

☐ **TIME**
An hour or two for most repairs

☐ **TOOLS**
Two pipe wrenches, groove-joint pliers

☐ **SKILLS**
Testing for a gas leak, tightening connections

☐ **PREP**
Locate all gas shutoff valves so you know how to quickly turn off the gas.

☐ **MATERIALS**
Yellow pipe thread tape, new gas flexible connector

SAFETY FIRST
Handling a gas emergency

If you smell gas in your home, take no chances. Have your family leave immediately. Shut off the gas at the meter and open windows and doors. Contact the gas company immediately to come and inspect your home.

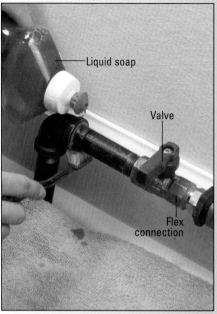

1 To test for a leak, spray gas-joint testing fluid, or brush liquid soap (shown) or soapy water on a suspect joint. If you see bubbles, there is a leak. Tightening the nipple or valve will likely stop the leak. Note that a flex connection installed in the last 10 years will have left-hand threading.

2 If the leak is at a black gas line, **shut off gas to the line**. Disassemble the pipes. Clean away any existing pipe-joint compound from the threads and wrap each end with several windings of yellow thread tape made especially for gas lines. Use pipe wrenches to tighten each piece firmly.

Appliance shutoff

Every gas appliance should have a nearby shutoff valve. To shut off gas to the appliance, turn the handle until it is perpendicular to the pipe.

Copper pipe for gas lines?
Copper pipe has been used for gas lines in the past, but gas causes the inside of the pipe to flake, damaging gas appliances.

Gas shutoff valve

A house shutoff is usually located on the gas meter. To shut off gas to the entire house, turn the valve slowly a quarter-turn with a pipe wrench. To make sure no one turns the gas back on, padlock the valve.

REPAIRS TO CAST-IRON PIPE

Old cast-iron drainpipe can behave unpredictably. Sometimes a small section of a pipe starts to crumble or a joint begins to leak even though most of the pipe is sound.

If a cast-iron pipe is failing at several points, the most economical solution is to replace it with PVC pipe. This is a job for a professional.

Older cast-iron joints were sealed with molten lead, but this is not a danger to your health, since only wastewater passes through the pipes.

PRESTART CHECKLIST

☐ **TIME**
An hour or two to install a clamp around a damaged area

☐ **TOOLS**
Screwdriver, adjustable wrench, wire brush, hammer, cold chisel, putty knife

☐ **SKILLS**
Assembling a clamp and tightening screws

☐ **PREP**
Make sure that the pipe is well supported.

☐ **MATERIALS**
Repair paste or plumber's epoxy

SAFETY FIRST
Support cast-iron pipe

Cast-iron pipe is very heavy and must be held in place with special clamps attached to framing members. Never disturb these clamps; if one weakens, a long section of pipe could come crashing down.

Cold chisel

1 If water or a bad smell comes from an old leaded joint, use a cold chisel and hammer to gently tap the lead back into the joint. Use a wire brush and rag to clean away the corrosion.

2 Fill the resulting void with cast-iron pipe repair paste. Use a putty knife to apply the paste.

WHAT IF…
A cast-iron pipe has a hole?

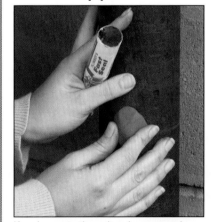

If a pipe rusts through or is punctured, clean the opening with a wire brush and fill the hole with two-part plumber's epoxy. Check the manufacturer's instructions for drying time. Don't use the pipe until the patch has completely set.

STANLEY PRO TIP

Replacing a section of cast-iron pipe

If more than a small area is damaged, this is a job for a professional. Hire a plumber to cut out a section of the pipe and replace it with PVC pipe.

First, the pipe must be supported both below and above the area to be removed. At least one new pipe clamp must be installed. It may be necessary to build a wooden frame and attach the clamp to it.

Once the pipe is cut, a section of PVC pipe is attached at both ends to the cast-iron pipe using neoprene sleeves. After the installation is complete, you may or may not be able to remove the new clamp, depending on the situation.

LEAKS AT STOP VALVES AND SUPPLY TUBES

If water is dripping onto the floor of a cabinet below a sink, leaky supply pipes may be the cause. More likely, however, a stop valve or supply-tube connection is the culprit.

To find the source of a leak, shine a bright flashlight into the cabinet and feel the pipes and tubes, stopping to dry your hand every so often. You can also dry the area, place dry newspaper under the suspect plumbing, and watch for spots of water.

A solid chrome-plated copper supply tube looks and feels more stable than a flexible braided tube. But the solid tube is actually more likely to develop a leak because it is inflexible. When bumped, a braided tube is less likely to be damaged. Still, many people prefer the appearance of a solid tube.

PRESTART CHECKLIST

☐ **TIME**
Less than an hour to tighten nuts or install a new supply tube

☐ **TOOLS**
Adjustable wrench, groove-joint pliers, basin wrench, tubing cutter, tubing bender

☐ **SKILLS**
Measuring and cutting a tube, connecting a compression fitting

☐ **PREP**
Place a bucket or towel below the leaking plumbing. Make the area comfortable for working.

☐ **MATERIALS**
Solid or braided supply tube

Tightening stop valve connections

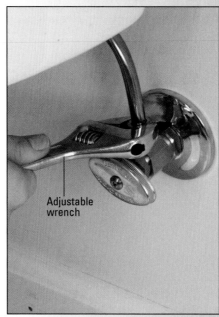

Adjustable wrench

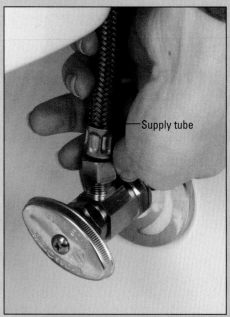

Supply tube

1 If water leaks at the stop-valve spout, use an adjustable wrench to tighten the nut that connects the supply tube to the valve. (If valve moves at all, brace it with another wrench.) If water leaks from where the supply tube enters the faucet, tighten the nut with a basin wrench.

2 If that doesn't solve the problem, **shut off the water** at the stop valve. Unscrew the nuts at either end and remove the supply tube. Replace with a flexible braided tube or install a new solid supply tube *(page 109)*.

Stop-valve quality

An inexpensive stop valve (bottom) has plastic inner parts, making it more likely to break down. Its inner parts must be removed before sweating. The more substantial unit (top) has all-metal inner parts that are long-lasting and don't need to be removed before sweating.

A stop valve has a stem much like that in a compression faucet. The packing washer and stem washer can be replaced, but it's easier to simply replace the entire valve.

Replacing a solid supply tube

1 Bend a chrome-plated copper or plain copper supply tube carefully by hand or use a tubing bender *(page 99)*.

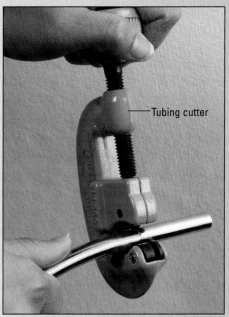

Tubing cutter

2 Insert one end of the tube into the faucet inlet above, hold the other end near the stop valve, and mark it for a cut. Make the cut with a tubing cutter. (See *page 98* for how to use a tubing cutter).

Nut

Ferrule

3 At the upper end, slip on the mounting nut and a ferrule. Poke the tube into the faucet inlet, slide the ferrule up to the inlet, and tighten the nut. Slip a nut and ferrule onto the lower end of the tube and attach to the stop valve in the same way.

STANLEY PRO TIP

Buy the right supply tube

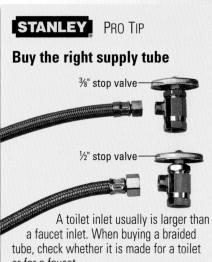

⅜" stop valve

½" stop valve

A toilet inlet usually is larger than a faucet inlet. When buying a braided tube, check whether it is made for a toilet or for a faucet.

Stop valves have spouts that are either ½ inch or ⅜ inch in diameter (above). Be sure to buy a tube made to fit your valve.

A common mistake is to buy a supply tube that is too short. Play it safe and buy a tube that's longer than you think you need.

WHAT IF...
You use a plastic supply tube?

A plastic supply tube seals using a ball-shaped end held firmly by a nylon nut. Some have a rubber ferrule as well.

Kink-proof solid supply tubes

These solid supply tubes bend without kinking. One is chrome-plated metal with a plastic liner to prevent kinks; the other is ribbed so it can be bent easily.

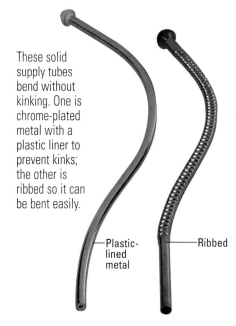

Plastic-lined metal

Ribbed

INSTALLING A STOP VALVE ON COPPER PIPE

Every faucet and toilet in a home should have its own stop valve so you can easily make repairs. Installing one is usually not difficult, though you may find yourself working in cramped quarters.

Take care to buy the correct valve. Its inlet must accommodate the size of pipe coming from the wall (usually ½-inch but sometimes ¾- or ⅜-inch). Its threaded spout must match the size of the supply tube—either ½- or ⅜-inch. You can install either a compression or a sweatable valve.

If the pipes are plastic, simply cut with a close-work hacksaw and cement the valve in place *(pages 102–103)*.

To shut off the water where there is no existing stop valve, see *page 7*. Some water will remain in the pipes and tubes after water has stopped flowing out the faucet, so place a bucket and towel underneath.

PRESTART CHECKLIST

☐ **TIME**
One or two hours to install a new stop valve in copper pipe

☐ **TOOLS**
Close-work hacksaw, two adjustable wrenches, propane torch

☐ **SKILLS**
Cutting and joining copper pipe

☐ **PREP**
Shut off the water and drain the line. Place a bucket or towel below the pipe to be cut.

☐ **MATERIALS**
New compression or sweatable stop valve, flux, solder, possibly a new supply tube

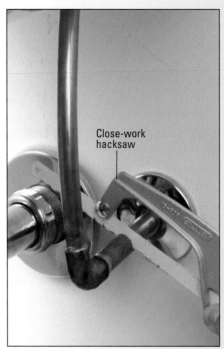

Close-work hacksaw

1 **Shut off the water** to the line and drain the line by turning on a faucet at a lower location. If there is room, cut the copper pipe using a tubing cutter. Otherwise cut slowly and gently with a close-work hacksaw, as shown.

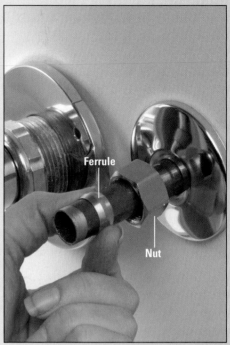

Ferrule

Nut

2 Sand the outside of the cut pipe with a combination wire brush, emery cloth, or sandpaper until it is shiny. Slide a nut and ferrule onto the pipe.

STANLEY PRO TIP

Use two wrenches

Adjustable wrench

Slide the stop valve all the way onto the pipe. Hold the valve with one adjustable wrench while you tighten the nut with the other.

WHAT IF...
You use a sweatable valve?

Before sweating a valve, protect the wall or cabinet from the flame with pieces of sheet metal. Remove the valve's inner parts and follow sweating instructions and safety tips on *pages 98–101*. Wait for the valve to cool before reassembling.

INSTALLING A STOP VALVE ON STEEL PIPE

If an old galvanized pipe comes out from the wall, installing a shutoff valve is usually a straightforward job; simply screw a threaded stop valve onto the pipe.

If possible, unscrew the supply tube at the bottom only, so it remains attached to the faucet or toilet above. If this is not possible, you may have to cut through the supply tube with a hacksaw and replace the tube after installing the valve.

Unscrew the parts up to the nipple that sticks out of the wall. Look into the pipe with a flashlight. If it is partially filled with mineral deposits, replacing it will increase the faucet's (or toilet's) water pressure.

To shut off the water where there is no existing stop valve, see *page 7*. Some water will remain in the pipes and tubes after water has stopped flowing out the faucet, so you might want to place a bucket or a thick towel underneath.

PRESTART CHECKLIST

☐ **TIME**
One or two hours to install a new stop valve in galvanized-steel pipe

☐ **TOOLS**
Two pipe wrenches, adjustable wrench, or groove-joint pliers

☐ **SKILLS**
Cutting and joining steel pipe

☐ **PREP**
Shut off the water and drain the line. Place a bucket or towel below the pipe to be cut.

☐ **MATERIALS**
New threaded stop valve for your size of pipe, pipe-thread tape, possibly a pipe nipple

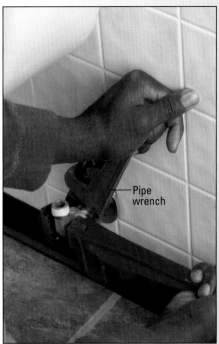

1 **Shut off the water** and drain the line by turning on a faucet at a lower location. Hold the steel pipe still with one pipe wrench while you remove the elbow with another pipe wrench. If you cannot budge the elbow, slip a length of 1¼-inch steel pipe on it for more leverage.

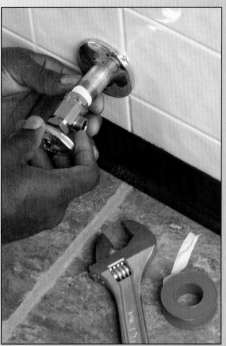

2 Clean the pipe threads and wrap pipe-thread tape clockwise around the threads several times. Screw the stop valve onto the pipe and tighten with an adjustable wrench. (Don't crank hard with a pipe wrench or the valve might crack.)

REFRESHER COURSE
Working with steel pipe

Measure to find the pipe lengths you need; take into account the distance the pipes will travel inside fittings and valves.

Wrap each pipe end with several windings of pipe-thread tape and use a pipe wrench to firmly tighten each pipe and fitting in order. Tighten with a tool no smaller than a 14-inch pipe wrench; a smaller tool may not have enough power.

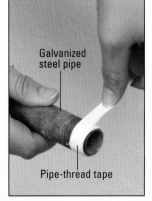

Match supply tubes with stop valves.
Stop valves have spouts that are either ½-inch or ⅜-inch diameter. Buy supply tubes to fit the valves and faucet connection.

REPAIRING SHUTOFF VALVES

Sometimes it's inconvenient to replace a shutoff valve, so it makes more sense to at least attempt a repair.

To shut off water ahead of the valve, see *page 7*.

If water leaks from the packing nut (just under the handle), tighten it with groove-joint pliers. Don't crank too hard or you may crack it. If that doesn't stop the leak, disassemble the valve and replace the packing washer or thread packing.

If the valve does not shut water off completely, dismantle and replace any worn parts.

PRESTART CHECKLIST

☐ **TIME**
Less than an hour for most repairs

☐ **TOOLS**
Screwdriver, adjustable wrench, groove-joint pliers, soft wire brush

☐ **SKILLS**
Dismantling and replacing small parts

☐ **PREP**
Shut off water to the valve, and open faucets to at least partially drain the line.

☐ **MATERIALS**
Replacement parts for the valve

Packing nut
Stem

Replacement packing washer

1 **Shut off the water** and drain the line. Use an adjustable wrench to unscrew the packing nut; pull out the stem.

2 Slowly turn water back on and flush out any debris, then turn it off again. Check the inside of the valve body for debris and clean with a soft wire brush if necessary.

3 Replace a washer or any other rubber part with a duplicate. If needed, wrap new packing thread around the stem *(page 39)* and push it up into the packing nut. Reassemble and tighten the packing nut.

HOSE BIB, GATE VALVE, AND GLOBE VALVE

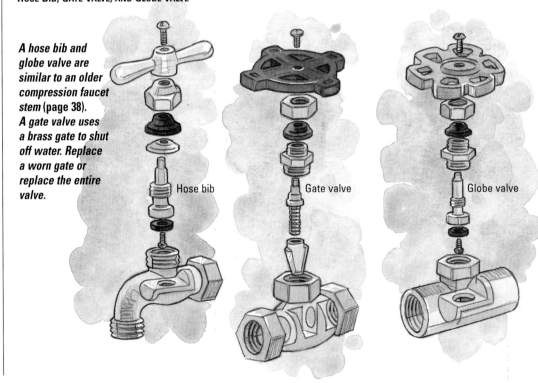

A hose bib and globe valve are similar to an older compression faucet stem (page 38). A gate valve uses a brass gate to shut off water. Replace a worn gate or replace the entire valve.

Hose bib

Gate valve

Globe valve

SILENCING PIPE NOISES

Pipes that rattle and hammer are not only annoying, they also may eventually come apart at the joints. Take steps to stop the noise and prevent possible leaks.

The most common noise is water hammer, a rattle that occurs when water is turned on or off by a faucet or an appliance, such as a dishwasher or clothes washer. The solution is to install a shock absorber, also called an air chamber, which provides a cushion to dampen the water's movement.

The following instructions show how to install a shock absorber using threaded fittings. See *page 16* for a type that can be sweated onto a copper system. You can also fabricate one for plastic pipe using a piece of pipe and a cap fitting; see *pages 102–103* for instructions on gluing.

After a few years, the air chamber may fill with water and lose its ability to soften water hammer. Draining and refilling the line will replenish the chamber with a cushion of air.

PRESTART CHECKLIST

☐ **TIME**
An hour or so to install a pipe shock absorber

☐ **TOOLS**
Tools for working with copper *(page 98)*, with plastic pipe *(page 102)*, or with steel pipe *(page 104)*

☐ **SKILLS**
Cutting and joining copper, plastic, or steel pipe

☐ **PREP**
Shut off the water and drain the line.

☐ **MATERIALS**
Shock absorber for your type and size pipe, materials for joining the pipe

1 **Shut off water** and drain the line. Measure the shock absorber to determine how much pipe must be cut out; remember that pipe will be inserted into the absorber at each end. Cut the pipe with a tubing cutter, if possible; otherwise saw carefully with a hacksaw.

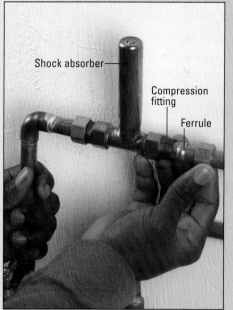

2 On each side of the absorber location, slip a compression nut on the pipe, threaded side toward the absorber, then slip on a ferrule. On each side of the shock absorber, push the nut over the ferrule and finger-tighten the joint. Use an adjustable wrench to complete the installation.

Adding pipe insulation

A pipe may vibrate when water runs through it, causing it to rattle against a nearby framing member. Cushion the pipe by slipping on foam insulation pieces. Firm up loose pipes with pipe clamps or hanger brackets.

WHAT IF...
There is no access to pipes?

This type of shock absorber is made for use in a laundry room. Simply detach each washer hose from its hose bib, screw on the shock absorber, and attach each hose.

THAWING PIPES AND WINTERIZING

Pipes that are not sufficiently insulated may freeze during cold weather. The result could be a minor inconvenience—the pipes may be undamaged and the water will flow again when they thaw out. Or it could be a major catastrophe in the form of a burst pipe. Take steps now rather than later to protect them.

Exposed pipes are easily insulated or heated (right). If the pipes are inside a wall, the job may be difficult. If the exterior wall is the inside wall of an attached garage, consider attaching solid foam insulation on the garage side of the entire wall. Otherwise you'll have to remove the exterior or interior wall covering (whichever is easier), insulate the pipes, and then reinstall the wall covering.

If the weather forecast calls for extreme cold and you fear that a pipe may freeze, open a faucet or two on the line just a crack, so water comes out in a little more than a drip. Moving water freezes more slowly than still water.

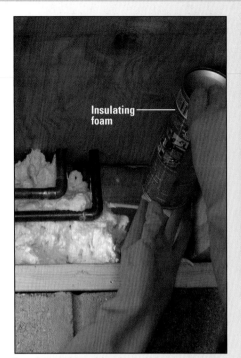

Insulate vulnerable pipes: Wrap exposed pipes with sections of foam insulation *(page 113)* or fill the surrounding area with fiberglass batts, loose-fill cellulose, or spray foam (shown). Leave part of the pipe exposed to warm, interior air.

Install heat tape: Newer types of electric pipe-heating tape are easy to install and turn themselves on only when needed. Wrap the tape around the pipe and plug the unit into a reliable electrical receptacle. Follow the manufacturer's instructions. Never overlap electric heat tape.

PRESTART CHECKLIST

☐ **TIME**
An hour or two to protect exposed pipes; much more time to protect pipes behind walls

☐ **TOOLS**
Portable heater, hair dryer, or heat gun; carpentry tools if you need to get at hidden pipes; caulking gun

☐ **SKILLS**
Identifying and locating the pipes that need to be protected

☐ **PREP**
Check the history of freezing pipes in your home; locate the vulnerable ones.

☐ **MATERIALS**
Insulation (various types), caulk, electric pipe-heating tape

WHAT IF...
Your pipes freeze?

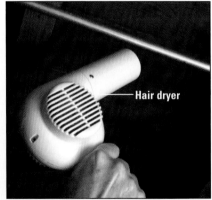

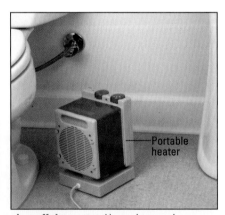

When water stops flowing during cold weather, you know that at least one pipe has frozen. (If only the hot water flows, you know the cold-water pipe has frozen.) A frozen pipe may or may not crack; you'll find out only after the water thaws. Just in case, watch the pipes continually and **be prepared to**

shut off the water. Have pipe repair materials on hand. If a pipe is exposed, thaw it by pointing a hair dryer or heat gun at it (left). (Don't get too close with the heat gun, and watch carefully for any drip or spray of water.) If the pipe is hidden in a wall, aim a portable heater at the area (right).

WINTERIZING A CABIN

If a cabin will be left unheated during the winter, take steps to prevent pipe damage due to freezing water. In addition to the steps shown, turn off the main shutoff valve and open a pipe nearby to let water drain out. Drain all water-using appliances, such as the dishwasher and clothes washer. If the cabin has hot-water heat, drain the heating system. Some cabins have small drain valves on the pipes; open them.

At the electrical service panel, shut off power to an electric water heater.

If the water heater is gas, shut off the gas that runs to it.

Even after draining the system, water will remain in traps. Pour about 3 cups of full-strength antifreeze into every toilet bowl.

Pour about a cup of antifreeze into each sink.

After shutting off power or gas, drain the water heater.

Drain hose bib

Pour about 2 cups of antifreeze into every shower and floor drain trap.

Drain each accessible trap before adding antifreeze.

Drain each stop valve.

Drain well pump.

Protect your outdoor hose bib with an indoor shutoff valve

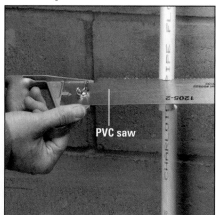

PVC saw

1 Using a PVC saw or scissors-type PVC cutters *(page 103)*, cut out a section of pipe. Take into account the fact that the pipes will slide into the valves at each side. Remove burrs from the pipes *(page 102)*.

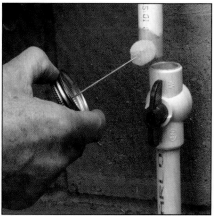

2 Make sure the valve fits. Apply primer outside the pipe and inside the valve. Cement one pipe and one side of the valve. Immediately slip the valve onto the pipe. Give it a slight twist and hold it for 30 seconds. Glue the other side.

Hose bib insulator

When cold weather approaches, disconnect and drain all outdoor hoses. Protect the outdoor faucet (called a hose bib or sill cock) by shutting off the water that runs to it and opening it. To protect it further, strap on a foam insulator like this one. For a long term solution, install an extended sill cock whose valve is indoors, protected from freezing conditions.

GLOSSARY

For terms not included here, or for more about those that are, refer to the index on *pages 118–120*.

ABS: One of the first plastic drain pipes used in homes, ABS (acrylonitrile-butadiene-styrene) is now forbidden in many municipalities in favor of PVC drain pipe.

Access panel: A removable panel in a wall or ceiling that permits repair or replacement of concealed items such as faucet bodies.

Adapter: A fitting that makes it possible to go from male endings to female endings or vice-versa. Transition adapters allow for joining different kinds of pipe together in the same run. Trap adapters help connect drainlines to a sink or lavatory trap.

Aerator: A device screwed to the spout outlet of most lavatories and sinks that mixes air with the water, which results in less water splash and smoother flow.

Auger: A flexible metal cable fished into traps and drainlines to dislodge obstructions.

Ballcock: The assembly inside a toilet tank that when activated releases water into the bowl to start the flushing action, then prepares the toilet for subsequent flushes. Also called a flush valve.

Basket strainer: A drain fitting on kitchen sinks that prevents debris from flowing into the drain and can be rotated so the sink can be filled.

Buffalo box: A type of whole-house shutoff where the valve is in a plastic or concrete box set in the ground.

CPVC: Heat-resistant and as strong as PVC, CPVC (chlorinated poly-vinyl-chloride) is approved by many municipalities for indoor supply lines.

Catch basin: An underground grease catchment connected to a drain. Catch basins are commonly bypassed or abandoned.

Cleanout: A removable plug in a trap or a drainpipe that allows easier access to blockages inside.

Closet bend: The elbow-shaped fitting beneath a toilet that carries waste to the main drain.

Codes: See Uniform Plumbing Code.

Compression fitting: A brass or plastic fitting used to join pipe by tightening two nuts that force a ring-like ferrule into the fitting to assure a tight seal.

Coupling: A copper, galvanized steel, plastic, or brass fitting used to connect two lengths of pipe in a straight run.

Dielectric fitting: This fitting joins copper and steel pipe. By means of a specially-designed plastic washer, it insulates the pipes from an otherwise corrosive chemical reaction. See also transition fitting.

Diverter: A valve on a faucet that changes the flow of water from a faucet spout to a hand sprayer or, on a tub/shower faucet, from the tub spout to the shower head.

Drain-waste-vent (DWV) system: The network of pipes and fittings that carries liquid and solid wastes out of a building and to a public sewer, a septic tank, or a cesspool, and allows for the passage of sewer gases to the outside.

Drum trap: Found in older homes, this cylindrical trap is built into the floor and covered with a brass, chrome-plated, or expandable cap.

Elbow: A fitting used to change the direction of a water supply line. Also known as an ell. Bends do the same thing with drain-waste-vent lines.

Fall: A word used to express the slope drain lines are installed at to ensure proper waste drainage. Minimum fall per foot is ¼ inch.

Fitting: Any connector (except a valve) that lets you join pipes of similar or dissimilar size or material in straight runs or at an angle.

Fixture: Any of several devices that provide a supply of water or sanitary disposal of liquid or solid wastes. Tubs, showers, sinks, lavatories, and toilets are examples.

Fixture drain: The drainpipe and trap leading from a fixture to the main drain.

Flux: A stiff jelly brushed or smeared on the surfaces of copper and brass pipes and fittings before joining them to assist in the cleaning and bonding processes.

I.D.: The abbreviation for inside diameter. All plumbing pipes are sized according to their inside diameter. See also O.D.

Main drain: That portion of the drainage system between the fixture drains and the sewer drain. See also fixture drain and sewer drain.

Nipple: A 12-inch or shorter pipe that has threads on both ends and that is used to join fittings. A close nipple has threads that run from both ends to the center.

Nominal size: The designated dimension of a pipe or fitting. It varies slightly from the actual size.

O.D.: The abbreviation for outside diameter. See also I.D.

O-ring: A round rubber washer used to create a watertight seal, chiefly around valve stems.

PE: Flexible PE (polyethylene) supply pipe is the newest type of plastic pipe. Many codes restrict its use.

PVC: Polyvinyl-chloride (PVC) pipe is the most commonly accepted type of plastic drain pipe. PVC is sometimes also used for supply pipes, but most codes no longer allow it for hot water supply lines because heat causes it to shrink, weakening joints.

Packing: A plastic or metallic cord-like material used chiefly around faucet stems. When compressed it results in a watertight seal.

Pipe joint compound: A material applied to pipe threads to ensure a watertight or airtight seal. Also called pipe dope.

Pipe thread tape: A synthetic material wrapped around pipe threads to seal a joint.

Plumber's putty: A dough-like material used as a sealer. Often a bead of it is around the underside of toilets and deck-mount sinks and lavatories.

P.S.I.: The abbreviation for pounds per square inch. Water pressure is rated at so many PSIs.

Reducer: A fitting with different size openings at either end used to go from a larger to a smaller pipe.

Riser: A pipe supplying water to a location or a supply tube running from a pipe to a sink or toilet.

Rough-in: The early stages of a plumbing project during which supply and drain-waste-vent lines are run to their destinations. All work done after the rough-in is finish work.

Run: Any length of pipe or pipes and fittings going in a straight line.

Saddle tee valve: A fitting used to tap into a water line without having to cut the line apart. Some local codes prohibit its use.

Sanitary fitting: Any of several connectors used to join drain-waste-vent lines. Their design helps direct wastes downward.

Sanitary sewer: Underground drainage network that carries liquid and solid wastes to a treatment plant.

Septic tank: A reservoir that collects and separates liquid and solid wastes, then digests the organic material and passes the liquid waste onto a drainage field.

Sewer drain: That part of the drainage system that carries liquid and solid wastes from a dwelling to a sanitary sewer, septic tank, or a cesspool.

Shock absorber: A device that provides a cushion of air to prevent water hammer.

Soil stack: A vertical drainpipe that carries wastes toward the sewer drain. The main soil stack is the largest vertical drain line of a building into which liquid and solid wastes from branch drains flow. See also vent stack.

Stop valve: A device installed in a water supply line, usually near a fixture, that lets you shut off the water supply to one fixture without interrupting service to the rest of the system. Stop valves are built into some tub/shower faucets.

Storm sewer: An underground drainage network designed to collect and carry away water coming into it from storm drains. See also sanitary sewer.

Sweating: A technique used to produce watertight joints between copper pipe and fittings. A pipe and fitting are cleaned, coated with flux, and pushed together. When the fitting is heated to the proper temperature with a torch, solder is drawn into the joint by capillary action to make the seal.

Tailpiece: That part of a fixture drain that bridges the gap between the drain outlet and the trap.

Tee: A T-shaped fitting used to tap into a length of pipe at a 90-degree angle for the purposes of beginning a branch line.

Transition fitting: Any one of several fittings that joins pipe made of dissimilar materials, such as copper and plastic, plastic and cast iron, or galvanized steel and copper.

Trap: Part of a fixture drain required by code that creates a water seal to prevent sewer gases from penetrating a home's interior.

Uniform Plumbing Code: A nationally recognized set of guidelines prescribing safe plumbing practices. Local codes take precedence over it.

Union: A fitting used in runs of threaded pipe to facilitate disconnecting the line (without ever having to cut it).

Vent: The vertical or sloping horizontal portion of a drain line that permits sewer gases to rise out of the house. Every fixture in a house must be vented.

Vent stack: The upper portion of a vertical drain line through which gases pass directly to the outside. The main vent stack is the portion of the main vertical drain line above the highest fixture connected to it through which sewer gases from various fixtures escape upward and to the outside.

Water hammer: A loud noise caused by a sudden stop in the flow of water, which causes pipes to repeatedly hit up against a nearby framing member.

Water supply system: The network of pipes and fittings that transports water under pressure to fixtures and other water-using equipment and appliances.

Wet wall: A strategically place cavity (usually a 2×6 wall) in which the main drain/vent stack and a cluster of supply and drain-waste-vent lines are housed.

Y: A Y-shaped drainage fitting that serves as the starting point for a branch drain supplying one of more fixtures.

INDEX

METRIC CONVERSIONS

U.S. Units to Metric Equivalents			Metric Units to U.S. Equivalents		
To convert from	Multiply by	To get	To convert from	Multiply by	To get
Inches	25.4	Millimeters	Millimeters	0.0394	Inches
Inches	2.54	Centimeters	Centimeters	0.3937	Inches
Feet	30.48	Centimeters	Centimeters	0.0328	Feet
Feet	0.3048	Meters	Meters	3.2808	Feet
Yards	0.9144	Meters	Meters	1.0936	Yards
Square inches	6.4516	Square centimeters	Square centimeters	0.1550	Square inches
Square feet	0.0929	Square meters	Square meters	10.764	Square feet
Square yards	0.8361	Square meters	Square meters	1.1960	Square yards
Acres	0.4047	Hectares	Hectares	2.4711	Acres
Cubic inches	16.387	Cubic centimeters	Cubic centimeters	0.0610	Cubic inches
Cubic feet	0.0283	Cubic meters	Cubic meters	35.315	Cubic feet
Cubic feet	28.316	Liters	Liters	0.0353	Cubic feet
Cubic yards	0.7646	Cubic meters	Cubic meters	1.308	Cubic yards
Cubic yards	764.55	Liters	Liters	0.0013	Cubic yards

To convert from degrees Fahrenheit (F) to degrees Celsius (C), first subtract 32, then multiply by ⅝.

To convert from degrees Celsius to degrees Fahrenheit, multiply by ⅝, then add 32.